JESUS FREES US

The battle cry of a soldier for
Christ

Shane Murray

JESUS FREES US

Written by Shane Murray

Copyright © 2020 by Shane Murray.

All Scripture quotations are taken from the Holy Bible: Christian Standard Bible. CSB translation.

All emphasis added to Scripture quotations are the author's.

Editing was done by Art Kelly, Debbie Lock and Shanna Leasure.

Also available in e-book format.

Printed in the United States of America
2020

To my beautiful bride Halee. To Eli and Emslee, the two best children a father could have. To all of the men in my group that I call brothers. To their families that have become my family in Christ. To Jesus Christ who saved my soul. To the Holy Spirit who directs my path. To God the Father who called me out of darkness. This is a collective work that would not have been possible without you.

Presented To:

From:

CONTENTS

Introduction.. 7

Chapter 1: New Creation............................ 11

Chapter 2: A Fire In My Bones.................... 23

Chapter 3: Removing The Mask................. 39

Chapter 4: Renew Your Mind...................... 53

Chapter 5: Divine Appointments.............. 67

Chapter 6: What's It Worth?......................... 81

Chapter 7: Freedom....................................... 93

Chapter 8: Community................................. 109

Chapter 9: Intimacy With Christ.............. 123

Chapter 10: Saving Faith............................ 139

Chapter 11: Finishing Well........................ 157

INTRODUCTION

I've called myself a Christian my whole life. My grandfather was a preacher and a missionary. My mom took us to church on and off growing up, so I knew who Jesus was and what He did for me. However, it wasn't until age 23 that I truly started following Christ.

I did a lot of horrible things as a preteen, teenager, and young adult. I didn't realize that the sin habits I formed in my youth would plague me into adulthood. When I started to follow Christ, it became apparent that many of the things I thought were merely bad habits or choices, were so much more than that. They had actually attached themselves to me in a way that became strongholds in my life. I wasn't only serving my flesh, I was a slave to it. Maturing in my faith, I have come to realize that there is a battle-waging war not only all around me, but on the inside as well.

If we are going to be in a war, then we better learn how to fight. *"The weapons of our warfare are not of the flesh, but are powerful through God for the demolishing of strongholds." 2 Corinthians 10:4.* Through Christ, we have access to power that not only saves, but also transforms and renews. His power is able to demolish strongholds and bring freedom!

At the age of 23, I examined my life and realized I was a hypocrite. I had claimed to be a Christian my entire life while living like hell for the majority of it. This began a period of reading through the Bible to determine if I truly believed what it said. I had decided that if it proved to be true, then I would give my life to Christ and live for Him. If it proved to be false, I would stop claiming to be something I'm not. It was during that year of reading through the Bible that God grabbed hold of my life in a very real way. He began to speak to me through His Word. I began to see internal changes that resulted in a new way of living. Years later, I got invited to a retreat during a low point in my life following a job loss. What I encountered that weekend gave me the idea for something that would end up truly bringing freedom to my life and to many others lives as well.

Many people claim to be Christians, but have no clue what it means to follow Christ. Many who claim the name of Jesus don't know what it means to be free. My hope is that in the pages of this book you will have a renewed perspective on what it looks like to overcome the flesh and walk in the Spirit.

Jesus Frees Us is a battle cry for a soldier in Christ. It is the acknowledgment that we are in a battle that calls us to action, and there is victory in Him. It is a declaration of freedom and unity. Throughout this book are several testimonies of people who have found lasting and life changing freedom through Jesus. My hope is that you will find encouragement and strength to live a life in humble submission to the King of kings, while fighting the good fight of faith that brings freedom to every area of your life.

JESUS FREES US

"Being 'born again' is not a change of my name, but a renewal of my nature."

Charles Spurgeon

1

New Creation

"Therefore, if anyone is in Christ, he is a new creation; the old has passed away, and see, the new has come!"
2 Corinthians 5:17

What does it mean to be a new creation? There's a guy I know who had what I call a *Damascus Road* experience. If you are not familiar with that term, look up Acts 9:1-22. There you will find the story of a Jewish Pharisee named Saul who went from being zealous for the Law and persecuting Christians to becoming one. Saul was on his way to a town called Damascus with the intent to capture and imprison followers of Christ when a bright light came from heaven that knocked him off of his horse and blinded him. Jesus spoke to him through a thundering voice asking why he was persecuting Him. Saul asked, *"Who are you Lord?"* Jesus answered, *"I am Jesus, the one whom you are persecuting."* After that encounter with the living Christ, Saul went on to receive his sight back through a series of events and change his name to Paul. Paul went on to write the majority of our New Testament and preach the gospel of Jesus to Jews and non-Jews alike. In an instant, all things were new!

Unfortunately, that's not how it went for me. My transformation took a little longer, but was no less powerful. This walk with Jesus is a marathon, not a sprint, and it is something we will be growing in for the rest of our lives. As we intentionally walk out our faith in Christ day-to-day, reading His Word, spending time in prayer and applying His teachings to our daily lives, we grow closer and closer into His image. This is a process called *sanctification*. I will get into this term some more later on. For now I want to tell you a little about my life before Christ (B.C.) and how I became a *new creation*. (This term refers to the spiritual rebirth in Christ Jesus.)

A Little About Me

I remember when I was 11 years old and got baptized. I had been in church on and off through my youth. My grandfather on my mother's side was a preacher and a missionary. My grandmother and he lived in Florida but I grew up in Alabama, so we only saw each other on holidays or vacations. My mom would take us to different churches from time to time. We didn't have what you would call a church home, but we went enough for me to know the basics of Christianity. My dad never came with us on Sundays. He would drop us off or just stay home all together. Growing up, I didn't think real men went to church. However, a friend of mine was getting baptized and I wanted to follow suit. I knew Jesus died for my sins and was raised from the dead three days later. I knew it and I believed it, I just didn't understand that true belief was followed by a commitment to pursuing Him.

I got dunked in a tank at 11 years old and nothing changed. I talked the same, I thought the same, I sinned the same and I lived the same; but now I could do all those things and claim to be a *"Christian"*. So I continued to live a life full of people-pleasing, cussing, looking at pornography, taking things that didn't belong to me, smoking and thats just my preteen years. As I grew up and went to high school, the drugs came into play and alcohol became a huge necessity. Girls were just objects to be used and tossed away. Stealing was a way to make extra cash, and I was quite good at it. Pornography was becoming an ever increasing means of entertainment, and anything that would help me fit in was fair game no matter the cost. I did this all while still claiming the name of Christ.

By the age of 16 I had been arrested a couple

times for minor things, but at the age of 17 my life took a major turn. Looking back on it now, I can see God's fingerprints all over it. It was a stepping stone that helped me to get where I am today. Nonetheless, at the time it was the scariest thing I had ever faced. I decided to skip basketball practice and roam the hallways of the school one night. As I went into the classrooms, I discovered all kinds of electronics that I could take and sell. However, just the thrill of taking it and not getting caught was enough payment in and of itself. The following day, a detective came into my classroom and pulled me out of school. The next thing I knew, I was in handcuffs and on my way to the juvenile detention center.

The judge informed me that I could be tried as an adult facing up to 15 years in jail. My prayer life grew like never before that day. Isn't it odd how people don't acknowledge God throughout their lives, but when life gets rocky all of the sudden they expect Him to bail them out? Well that was me... I was praying and I had everyone I knew that believed in God praying for me.

When I went back to court to receive my sentence, the craziest thing happened. They called my name and I walked to the podium. The judge looked at me and told me that my arresting officer had not shown up to court that day. She stated that she believed I had learned my lesson and she would not see me back there again. She told me that I deserved to have my arresting officer show up, and since he didn't come to present his case against me, she was acquitting me of all charges and expunging it off of my record. I did the crime, and justly deserved to receive the punishment, yet I was given a second chance. Don't you know that our God is a God of second chances? *"For all have sinned and fall short of the glory of God. They are justified freely by His grace through the redemption that is in Christ Jesus." Romans 3:23,24.* Because of His goodness, we are made right with God through Christ's sacrifice! It's not anything that we have done ourselves, but it's God's grace.

You would think that God coming through for me like that would have been my big turning point, but it wasn't. I continued to live a life of sin. I did however stop stealing. That was a promise I made to God that I would stop if He got me out of the mess I was in, and I followed through on it. It's my personal belief that we can't make "deals" with God, but that's where I was at the time, and God graciously met me where I was at. One of the biggest blessings of my life, *(though I couldn't see it at the time)*, was that I was no longer able to attend the high school I was going to or hang out with the crowd that I used to run with. I later found out that several of the guys I ran with got locked up for murder and/or home invasions. I thank God that wasn't me!

"Do not be deceived: Bad company corrupts good morals."
1 Corinthians 15:33

My college life was filled with more hardcore drugs, more drinking, and more girls. The only thing that really changed was the crime side of my life. It wasn't until I turned 23 that things took what I like to call a "God-turn". At that time in my life, God really got a hold of my heart and literally began the process of transforming me into a new creation.

At age 23, I took a hard look at my life and realized that I was a hypocrite. Saying one thing and doing another. I called myself a Christian my whole life, but how I lived sure didn't reflect those values. I made a decision that I was going to read the Bible all the way through in a year, and then I would decide if I truly believed what it said. If so, then I would dedicate my life to Christ and live for Him. If not, then I would stop calling myself a Christian.

What God did in that year would change the course of my life forever. At first I had to make myself read everyday, but then it became something I couldn't go without. If I missed my Bible reading then my whole day was shot. It says in Scripture that the words contained in the Bible are "God-Breathed". Every time we read this book, we are breathing in His words and His life while also being filled up in our spirits with His Holy Spirit. As I read it day in and day out, the Word came alive to me. Every time I opened it, it was like He was somehow speaking directly to me. Pretty soon I was filling every waking moment I had with either the Bible, Christian books, sermons, prayer, or talking to people about my new found faith. I was on fire! It was like I was a different person, and the truth is that's because I was!

It says in Galatians 2:20, *"I have been crucified*

with Christ, and I no longer live, but Christ lives in me. The life I now live in the body, I live by faith in the Son of God, who loved me and gave Himself for me."

When God changes us, it is an inward change. We can read all of the self-help books and take all of the steps towards a better us possible, but if that change doesn't come from God working within us, then it is a band-aid at best. I once heard someone say, *"There's not 12 steps, there's one step and His name is Jesus."* I have seen the truth of that statement countless times throughout my life. I'm not trying to discount the application of practical steps in one's life to help overcome an addiction or better themselves as individuals. But apart from Jesus, your soul remains eternally damned and your years on earth lack true purpose. *"For what does it benefit a man to gain the whole world yet lose his soul?" Mark 8:36.* Jesus will rescue us from the pit of our infirmities as well as the pit of hell. Nothing is needed but a true encounter with Jesus Himself. It's not Jesus and _____. It's just Jesus!

A Spirit Exchange

A good friend of mine named Darren, who I do life with in my men's group is the epitome of a new creation. He grew up as a Jehovah's Witness (which is a cult that has many similarities to Christianity, but denies the deity of Jesus Christ, among other things). In his early teen years, he walked away from those beliefs as well as anything to do with God or religion. He wound up becoming a DJ in the rave scene and got into some pretty hardcore drugs.

My wife Halee, and his wife Shannon grew up together and have been best friends since 8 years old. Darren and his wife had been dating for 6 years and living together prior to his coming to faith in Jesus. In all that time, we had never hung out with him. Drinking was a huge part of their life as a couple. They lived together outside of marriage, and anytime she would mention hanging out with us, he would respond, *"I don't want to hang out with those bible thumpers!"* (We laugh about it now). The only thing Halee and I really knew about him was that he had issues with drugs, he drank a lot, he didn't want anything to do with church or God and he didn't want to get married or have kids. Shannon however, did want to get married and have a family.

Eventually, Shannon started coming to church with us from time to time. She wanted him to go, but that just wasn't an option. Their relationship was toxic and pretty soon she had had enough. She wanted to start pursuing Jesus and she also wanted to get married and have kids. Shannon knew that they were going down two completely different paths and it was time to split. That's when God started working on Darren. She told him it was over and she began the process of moving out. Until she could get her own apartment, she stayed in the guest bedroom of their home.

It was two weeks between then and his *Damascus Road* experience. During those two weeks, Darren prayed for the first time that he can remember. There were three nights leading up to his conversion that he woke up from the same dream crying out to God. In his dreams he was crying out, *"God please save me, God please save me!"* He would wake up each night saying that out loud with tears streaming down his face. On the third night, it was a little different. At the end of crying out *"God please save me"*, something scary happened. Right before being woke from his sleep, a demonic sounding voice came out that said, *"No, please don't go!"* He woke up in the middle of this creepy voice coming out of his own mouth. He was shaking in fear and didn't know what was going on.

The next morning, he went into the living room and found Shannon watching our church's sermon on the live YouTube broadcast. He asked her if he could watch it with her, and she was shocked. She immediately messaged Halee and said *"D is watching church with me in the living room"*. We didn't think much of it. I just assumed he was doing what he knew she wanted him to do. When the sermon ended Shannon messaged Halee again and said, *"We are on our way to the church, Darren wants to get baptized!"* I thought, *"Now hold on a second... He is taking this too far."* I asked Halee to get dressed. *"I've got to meet this guy!"* I said. Halee and I rushed up to the church and walked in right as He was getting out of the baptismal. He was crying like a baby and shaking like a leaf. I thought, *"Maybe this guy's legit"*, so I walked up and gave him a hug and told him congratulations. We decided to stay for the worship and then go to lunch and talk. The first song we sang was a worship song called *"No Longer Slaves"*. There is a line in that song that says, *"His blood runs through my veins."* At that moment in the song, I looked over at Darren to see him holding his tattooed forearms out and looking down at his veins through tear-filled eyes.

On the way out to the parking lot, he looked at me and said, *"Man you don't even know me, and you came up here to support me!"* Truth be told, I was coming up there to make sure he wasn't lying to Shannon. But we've been walking this out together ever since that day, and this guy is 100% authentic.

Shannon still moved out. They wanted to do things God's way this time. Now they are married and trying for a child. Darren is constantly sharing his faith with others, and living his life for the glory of God. He thinks a demon left him that third night when he woke up from his dream, and I think he's right. We believe that an "unholy" or "demonic" spirit left him. Shortly after this experience, Darren invited God, through His Holy Spirit to take up residence in his spirit. He reads the Bible more than anyone I know and he has this real relationship with Jesus that's evident. I am honored to call him my brother in Christ.

Stop Being Someone You Were Never Created To Be

Jesus frees us from who we were never intended to be in the first place. Because of "The Fall", mankind has been separated from God and enslaved to sin. Jesus came and broke the veil that divides us, granting us direct access to the Father. We now have the ability to approach the throne of God with grace and confidence.(Heb. 4:16) We no longer have to live as slaves to our flesh, we've been set free. Just as a butterfly is no longer considered a caterpillar, you *in* Christ are no longer *in* Adam. In Christ means to be saved, made new, reborn. In Adam is the fallen spiritual state of every person prior to their coming to Christ. Jesus not only offers forgiveness of sins, He gives us a whole new nature. No longer does the Father look at us in our fallen and sinful state, but in the righteousness of Christ. We can now live as children of God and heirs of His Kingdom because we are. We are new creations in Christ and free to live out the purpose that we were created for!

"What shall we say then? Shall we continue in sin so that grace may multiply? Absolutely not! How can we who died to sin still live in it? Or are you unaware that all of us who were baptized into Christ Jesus were baptized into His death? Therefore we were buried with Him by baptism into death, in order that, just as Christ was raised from the dead by the glory of the Father, so we too may walk in newness of life."
Romans 6:1-4

Jesus Frees Us

"Catch on fire with passion and people will come for miles to watch you burn."
John Wesley

2

A Fire In My Bones

"I say, "I won't mention him or speak any longer in his name." But his message becomes a fire burning in my heart, shut up in my bones. I become tired of holding it in, and I cannot prevail."
Jeremiah 20:9

I've heard it said before, *"The Holy Spirit is called the Comforter. Why would we need to experience the Comforter if our lives are already comfortable?"* When I heard that it was like a light bulb went off. I then started to do everything I could to get as far outside of my comfort zone as possible, and step into God's comfort zone.

I'm a huge introvert. Speaking to strangers or praying in front of others is extremely uncomfortable for me. However, I knew it was something that God was calling me to do. So I started going to prayer meetings every morning at my local church where all of these seasoned prayer warriors gathered. I would make myself pray in front of them, and I felt super inadequate. Nonetheless, I knew the more I practiced, the better I would get and the more comfortable it would be. I would fast during lunch on Wednesdays and go to a store parking lot to witness to strangers. Talk about uncomfortable... It was something I had to make myself go out and do, but I would always return with a huge amount of joy in knowing that God was smiling down on my feeble efforts. God had done something in me and I couldn't hold it in. Everyone needed to experience this, and I needed to tell them how.

I believe the biggest reason Christians don't share their faith more is because they fear a bad outcome. They either fear being rejected, or they fear not having the knowledge needed to answer the questions. The great thing about when God calls us to do something is that He isn't asking for success, He is only asking for obedience. God's Word clearly commands all Christ followers to share the good news of Jesus with the world around them. We are to be obedient to His commands and let the chips fall where they may. The outcomes are all up to God, that's His responsibility. David Wilkerson said it like this, *"When God calls you to something, He is not always calling you to succeed, He's calling you to obey! The success of the calling is up to Him; the obedience is up to you."* That takes all of the pressure off of me to succeed. It's so freeing to not be in charge of the outcomes.

Winning

I discovered a truth years ago that has helped me to get out of my comfort zone and face my fears. That truth is that when we share Jesus with someone, it's always a winning situation. There are only three things that can happen when sharing our faith. We can be rejected, we can plant a seed, or we can lead someone to Christ. The last two are obvious wins, it's always the first one that makes us apprehensive. That fear is put to rest when we shine the light of God's Word on it. Jesus said, *"Blessed are you when people hate you, when they exclude you, insult you and slander your name as evil because of the Son of Man. Rejoice in that day and leap for joy. Take note- your reward is great in heaven, for this is the way their ancestors used to treat the prophets." Luke 6:22-23.* Did you catch that? Jesus said that being rejected for His name is a win. Why? Because every time we are rejected for His name sake, we are storing up treasure in heaven! Treasure that will last forever unlike the stuff we buy here that will all one day be in a fire or a landfill.

Now that you can see how all outcomes are a winning situation when we share our faith, what are you waiting for? Go out and tell this lost and dying world the good news of Jesus!

Always on Mission

Last year, Halee and I went to the Dominican Republic with Darren and Shannon for a *honeymooniversary* trip. They had just gotten married, and it was mine and Halee's 8 year anniversary. We were there to hang out, have fun and relax. We weren't on a mission trip, we were at an all-inclusive resort. But when you allow God to guide your steps, everywhere is your mission field. One of the first guys we ran into at the resort went by the name of *"Mr. Dude"*. He was probably the most popular guy at the resort, everyone loved him. He was funny, he was handsome, and he was a smooth talker. He was a salesman for the many excursions they offered. We hit it off with him and let him know that if we decided to purchase any excursions, he would be our guy.

The next day we had to schedule our ride back to the airport for the end our stay with another salesman named Elvis. After making arrangements for the trip, we had to listen to his spiel about the deals on excursions and why we should purchase through him and not the other people at the resort. About halfway through his speech, Halee leans over to me and says,*"I want to ask him if he knows Jesus."* I said , *"Go for it!"* We sat there and listened to the rest of what he had to say and Halee told me she didn't see a good opening. I then said, *"Well I'm going to ask him then."* When he finished talking I said, *"Can I ask you a question? What do you think happens after you die, what's out there when we walk out of here?"* Now that's a good question for many reasons. First, it demands more than a one word answer. Second, it gets them thinking about eternity. Last, it doesn't throw the name Jesus in too soon. Jesus is a very powerful name, and if thrown into a conversation too early, it can shut the other person down.

Elvis proceeded to tell me that he believed in heaven but did not believe in hell. He also said that he believes the Bible to be true, but isn't religious. We had an amazing conversation, and we scheduled to meet him for a Bible study the next morning. Did you know that the Bible talks more about hell then it does about heaven; and it talks about it as a very real place. The next day, we had a wonderful time of Bible study with Elvis and got to pray with him. We don't know where that seed will end up harvesting, but we do know that God's Word never returns void. The outcome of that conversation is not up to us, it's up to God and we know He will use it for His glory.

After we left Elvis, we ended up crossing paths with *"Mr. Dude"*. If you have ever had a really good conversation about Jesus with a stranger, then you know how pumped you are right afterwards. That's how we felt right as we came across Mr. Dude. So the next thing you know, we are sitting on the beach with him talking about eternity and Jesus. He told us, *"Everyone from the United States I meet says that they are Christian, but you guys are Christian, Christian... Like real Christian!"* We talked about what it really means to believe in Jesus and how that decision shapes the way you live and view the rest of your life. What he was trying to say is that we took our beliefs seriously. And shouldn't we take Jesus seriously? I mean, He took us pretty serious when He hung from the cross and died for our sins. We ended up exchanging contact info with Mr. Dude whose real name is Michél, and have stayed in contact sending prayers and messages back and forth ever since.

Sharing Jesus was the highlight of our trip. The next guy was a young man selling merchandise on the beach to all of the tourists. When he walked up to our chairs, his eyes were crossed and foggy. You could tell he was partially blind. He was showing us all of these paintings that we later found out his brothers painted. He said that he walks to the beach everyday. It's a 2 hour trip each way to sell his brothers paintings and make money for their family. We didn't have as much money as he was initially trying to sell them for, but God tugged on Darren's heart to give him something. As this young man went through his paintings, he came across one and said it means good energy. Darren stopped him and said, *We don't believe in good energy, we believe in Jesus.* The man's eyes got really wide. He explained that he loves Jesus and was very strong in his beliefs. He told us that he never worries about if people will buy his paintings or not because God always provides no matter what. We encouraged him to be bold for Jesus and gave him the little bit of money that we had on us. Darren explained that it wasn't much, but we wanted him to have it and didn't want anything in return. The man tried giving us a painting in return for the money, but we wouldn't take it. His eyes were full of tears as he was rolling up the paintings in the sand. He looked up and said,

"Will you pray for my eyes?" We all got out of our chairs and laid hands on him as we prayed for God to bring healing to his eyes and to lead him by the power of His Holy Spirit down paths of righteousness. After praying we looked around and people were staring at us from all over the beach. We didn't get to witness the healing of his eyes that day, but we did get to witness God's love poured out and the joy that came in his heart from just talking to us.

"Love is not only something you feel, it is something you do."
David Wilkerson

Let me ask you a question... What are you obsessing over? What are you stressing about? Are you doing anything of significance beyond yourself? Is any of the stuff that fills your thought life eternally valuable? Let me tell you something. If it won't matter on the day you die, it shouldn't matter so much right now. If it won't matter in 5 years, it definitely shouldn't take up all this room in your mind! We spend so much time obsessing over things that don't even matter that we forget about things of true value. The only thing that will matter when you die is where you will spend eternity and what you did for Christ. Everything else will be burned up in the fire. If the most important thing in your life right now won't matter when you stand in front of the King, then adjust your perspective. Change your vantage point to where you can see through God's eyes. Then make the changes you need to live a kingdom lifestyle. One that will matter for eternity! How much of your life have you already wasted focusing on things that hold no weight? Haven't you wasted enough?

My Heart's Not Right With God

Allow me to tell you about a friend of mine who had an unexpected wake-up call that would change his life forever.

Josh is a young, good-looking, popular guy who had been in great health his entire life. He is fun, charming, successful, and someone everyone loves to be around. Not much mattered to him though unless it made him look good or made him money.

Josh grew up without a father figure. He was the oldest of three siblings whose mother worked two jobs just to make ends meet. They didn't have much as a family growing up, but they were always in church. That is where Josh met his godparents Dan and Thelma who loved him as their own. They often gave assistance to his mother without ever asking for anything in return. They were true examples of what selfless followers of Christ looked like. Dan was the dad that Josh never had and Thelma was mom #2.

Josh went through college as your typical student. Life was about drinking, drugs, girls and parties. He switched up majors constantly and made terrible grades until eventually getting expelled for plagiarism. Soon Josh met his wife Kenzie who helped him get his feet back underneath him. He eventually graduated with a degree in business.

Five years into their marriage, Kenzie was expecting their first child, Arlie Mae. On the day of delivery, they arrived at the hospital at 5:30am. When they walked through the doors, they saw Josh's godparents Dan and Thelma already there awaiting their arrival. 22 hours later, Arlie Mae arrived healthy and hungry. Dan and Thelma were the last ones to come in and see her, as the immediate family all took turns going back first. As soon as Thelma held Arlie in her arms, she began to cry tears of joy. Dan put his arm around Josh and told him, *"This is what it's all about. Now you will understand the love we have for you. Congratulations, she's beautiful!"* Before leaving, they all huddled in a circle as Dan prayed over them.

As Josh held Arlie in his arms and Kenzie went to sleep, the phone rang. His godfather was on the other end weeping bitterly. Thelma had a heart attack on the way home from the hospital and died. This experience wrecked Josh. He had experienced life and death all in the same day. The best day of his life quickly became the worst day of his life all at the same time.

Josh lashed out at God in anger crying out, *"How could You allow this happen? Why today?"* From that day forward, Josh was finished with God. He felt as if God must not exist because if He did, He would not have let this happen. The next three years of Josh's life consisted of no church, no prayer, and no relationship with the Lord.

With his wife Kenzie still being a Christian,

eventually they started attending one of their close friend's Bible studies. Josh only went to please his wife, and more so, to be an antagonist to their godly discussions and beliefs. He did everything in his power to express his sheer animosity towards God and to challenge their whole belief system.

Josh became a very successful businessman. He was self-employed which meant he got to be his own boss and could do things his own way. Josh found his value and worth through his performance and his money. His identity was based on the perception and opinions of others, and he would do almost anything to gain their approval. Personal gain was his top priority, and he pursued it at all costs. He would lie, cheat, exaggerate, betray, and swindle others to get whatever he wanted. He put his work, his business, and himself above everything and everyone. Though Josh had acquired a lot, he still found no contentment in all of his possessions. Rather than facing the emptiness, he would escape through drugs and alcohol. After a long day of work, he would separate himself from his family upon coming home. A typical night was spent out in their garage getting high and drinking until he passed out on the couch. This went on night after night as a continuous cycle of emptiness. He desperately needed change but was too consumed with himself to even realize it. That is, until Sunday, July 8th, 2018.

Josh was showing a client some properties on a hot summer day. All of the sudden he started feeling like he was going to pass out. Josh figured that is was a combination of the hot weather and an empty stomach. Nothing some AC and some food couldn't fix. He went and sat in his car with the AC blasting. Once he felt a little better he began his trip home. On the way home it happened again. He called his wife and told her that he thought he was going to pass out. She told him to pull over. Out of nowhere, all of his limbs started freezing up and paralysis took over. He jumped a median and wound up in a gas station parking lot. His muscles were contracted, and he couldn't move or even speak. People in the parking lot ran over to help. A nurse was there and said she thought he was having a stroke. The ambulance came and took Josh to the ER. While in the emergency room, things went back to normal. Then it happened again, only this time it was ten times worse.

At this point, Josh couldn't move, speak or even breathe on his own. The doctors were yelling, telling Josh to make himself breathe or they would have to stick a breathing tube down his throat. Then he began to pass out and felt like he was about to die. In that moment, all Josh can think of is, "I'm about to see Jesus, and he's going to tell me, 'Depart from me—I never knew you.'" He was scared to death. He began weeping and praying all kinds of selfish prayers in his head. He begged and pleaded and prayed with words he had never used before; "Lord Jesus, God, as I'm about to behold Your face, please forgive me! Please don't forsake me! Please have mercy on me! Please grace me with unearned reconciliation! Please let me into Your Kingdom! I'm so sorry for the way I've been and for the things I've done. Jesus, please help me!" He thought about his wife and daughter and earnestly prayed for them as well. His wife was going to be a widow, and his daughter was going to grow up just as he did—without a dad. It hurt knowing that his daughter would not understand, and his wife would not know just how much he loved and appreciated her. With the doctors running a breathing tube down his throat, Josh's vision began to blur and his heart began to flutter irregularly. With tear-filled eyes, darkness slowly consumed his sight until he was out.

Josh was in cardiac arrest for 17 seconds before being revived. Josh didn't die. He felt like he was about to, but he didn't. The diagnosis given by the doctors was Hypokalemia. The doctor told him that he was a miracle. After running all sorts of tests, it didn't make any sense. With the doctors and science unable to give Josh any real answers, he knew it had to be a God thing.

That event would change his life forever! That near-death experience put things into perspective for Josh. No longer would he put money, success and self as the priorities of his life. Moving forward, Josh wanted to know and be known by God. He wanted to have a real relationship with Jesus!

Ever since then, Josh has been passionate about pursuing Christ and loving people. He is probably the most genuinely loving guy that I know, and he wants everyone to know Jesus the way that he does now. Everything he owns, he holds with an open hand. He realizes that it's not his anyways; everything is God's.

One of the guys in our group was getting married and couldn't afford much, but wanted to give his bride her dream wedding. Josh and his wife Kenzie took all of the furniture out of their home and turned it into a wedding reception venue. They provided all of the food, decorations, etc. and hosted the whole thing at no cost to the bride or groom. That's just how their hearts work; they're givers. And shouldn't we all be givers if we are *in Christ*? God so loved the world that He *gave*... As His followers, we should adopt that same mentality.

I have seen Josh and his wife give their time, money, and love to anyone in need. A friend of ours was going through a rough separation with his wife, and Josh rearranged their home and lifestyle to accommodate him at their house. Josh is the kind of guy who makes you feel like you are the most important person in the world. It doesn't matter if there are ten of us in the room, he makes each of us feel the same way. He no longer lives for himself, but lives for the One who set him free. He has come to realize that only what honors God's name, advances His Kingdom, and accomplishes His will matters. I am eternally grateful for the opportunity to watch the transformation unfold in Josh's heart as he spreads Christ's love to all he encounters.

True Purpose

Jesus frees us from living an empty life. He gives our life true meaning and purpose. You and I were created with unique talents and gifts. God has prepared good works for you to do in advance that are specific to you. He has put his desires in your heart and a fire in your bones that you cannot hold back. The greatest life there is to live is one completely sold-out to Jesus!

Jesus Frees Us

"To be loved but not known is comforting but superficial. To be known and not loved is our greatest fear. But to be fully known and truly loved is, well, a lot like being loved by God. It is what we need more than anything. It liberates us from pretense, humbles us out of our self-righteousness, and fortifies us for any difficulty life can throw at us."

Timothy Keller

3

Removing The Mask

"Confess your sins to one another and pray for one another, so that you may be healed. The prayer of a righteous person is very powerful in its effect."
James 5:16

In today's society, it is normal to hide our faults and pretend everything is perfect at all times. We put our best foot forward and show the world our good side in our brightest moments and pretend like that's how it always is. We post pictures of our smiling kids and our new purchases on Facebook and Instagram to out-do the next person. We don't talk about the bribing it took to get our kids to sit still for that picture or mention the debt we just accrued over that new fully loaded SUV. When someone asks about our parenting techniques, we tell about the victories we have 1 out of 10 times. Everyone puts the highlights of their life on display. It's no wonder we feel like our lives don't measure up because it's just not real... It's a mask!

It's the same thing when it comes to our Christian walk. We see the victories in other people's lives and think they must never struggle like we do. We just assume that the difficulties and challenges that we face are individual to us. We tell ourselves, *"No one struggles with this the way I do, it's different for me..."* That is a lie from the devil and it reaps depression and anger as we buy into it and start believing it as truth.

1 Corinthians 10:13 tells us, *"No temptation has come upon you except what is common to humanity. But God is faithful; he will not allow you to be tempted beyond what you are able, but with the temptation he will also provide a way out so that you may be able to bear it."*

Stop Faking

Here's the truth. Everyone has struggles that they go through. We all deal with the same things. The lust of the flesh, the lust of the eyes, and the pride of life all wage war against our souls.(1 Jn. 2:16) We can choose to fight back with the weapons God gives us, or we can roll over and play the victim card saying, *"I can't handle it, it's too much, poor pitiful me."*

We tend to act a certain way in front of our Christian friends and leaders, and another way in front of non-believers or people that aren't as enthusiastic about their faith as we are. What if we no longer tried to put up a front to gain the approval of others? What if we lived for an audience of One? Instead, we often put on a "mask" and pretend like we don't struggle with anything serious when we're in front of other believers. Then we flip the "mask" over and refrain from bringing Jesus up around people that don't share our love for God.

What if we could find Christian brothers and sisters to confess our sins to? What if we prayed for one another and held each other accountable? What if we did life with other people serious about repentance and godly living? What if we encouraged each other to go deeper in our relationship with Christ? What if we pushed one another to step outside of our comfort zones and be intentional in living for the kingdom of God? We might actually start looking like the church according to the Bible. That's something so foreign to us because we always want to act like we have it all together.

On the flip-side of that is the way we put off talking about the most important thing in our life in an effort to be liked or accepted. If Jesus really is our all-in-all, then why don't we tell everyone about Him? Why is it that when we are around old friends that don't know about or share our faith in God, we shy away from the topic? They need Jesus too. If they're breathing, they need Jesus. Everyone you will ever meet needs Jesus. If we as Christians can't remove the mask and let our true self shine, then we are robbing the world around us of seeing Christ in us.

"You are the light of the world. A city situated on a hill cannot be hidden. No one lights a lamp and puts it under a basket, but rather on a lampstand, and it gives light for all who are in the house. In the same way let your light shine before others, so that they may see your good works and give glory to your Father in heaven."
Matthew 5:14-16

The Freedom To Be Real

Until a few years ago, I had never seen men get real about their struggles and show true godly love to other men in need. I had been pursuing Christ for a few years by now. I had seen the miraculous happen in and around me numerous times. I had watched God bring healing. I had watched prayers for people's health and salvation be answered. I had witnessed impossible situations made possible that can't be explained apart from God. But I had never seen men open up about serious challenges they were facing in their walk with Christ.

Many years ago, I was working a job that required a ridiculous amount of hours. I was working 70-100 hour weeks for three years straight. I didn't see my wife and kids much at all. My time for God was minimal, and I just wanted out. I started praying that God would help me to find a different job that would allow me more time for Him and my family.

Not long went by and I got a call from a company that I had never heard of. I hadn't even begun to send out resumes yet. They called and said they had heard about me and thought I would be a great addition to their team. They asked if I would come out to discuss taking a management position. It was the same type of business that I was in, but on a much smaller scale. From everything I could find online about the company, it didn't seem like it would be a realistic move. I thought that surely they wouldn't be able to pay me anything like what I was making, plus the drive was much further from home. Still, I felt compelled to go check it out.

When I went to meet them and tour the facility, something crazy happened. I spent over an hour of the interview talking about Jesus with the owner. We talked about what it meant to be a true follower of Christ and how God had flipped my life upside down recently. I explained that work was no longer my number one priority, but God and my family were. I laid out my convictions in full view straight out of the gate. By doing this, it held me accountable to live up to those convictions and not compromise my character for anyone.

The location was 4 times the distance from my house as my current job. The insurance was extremely more expensive, and they couldn't pay me close to what I was making. However, something just felt right. I switched jobs and began to see God move in a big way. I was getting to share Jesus with the people at my work without fear, and I saw many of the employees begin to draw near to God. There was only one problem. My direct boss hated me. He was a Mormon, and didn't like me shining God's truth on his false beliefs. Within my first year, he started making my life hell and I dreaded coming to work. It wasn't long before I got a call from another company that I had never heard of. Now God was showing off!

This time, the company was much closer to home and the pay was more than I had ever made. A lady who had worked for me at my previous job now worked there and told them about me. I landed the job and everything seemed perfect. It was like God just kept promoting me as I was faithful to what He was calling me to do.

The difference was that this time I didn't bring my faith with me to the office like I had previously done. I was still reading my Bible, praying, and sharing my faith at work, but not as much as before. I had laid out my non-negotiables very clearly from the start at my last job. This time, not so much. I was trying to hold onto the success I had attained by compromising on the very convictions that got me there in the first place. Now, instead of a dependence on God to sustain me, I was relying on my own abilities and letting life get in the way. I slowly stopped reading as much, my prayer life was weakening and soon I was giving into the flesh almost without hesitation. I had lost my first love. (Rev. 2:4) I was allowing the stresses of work and the busyness of life to distract me from what was truly important.

I stopped leading a small group for close to a year by this time and my fire was starting to die out. Satan had sunk his hooks back into me, and the flesh was winning the battle most days of the week. I knew something had to change. I went to my church to find a mens group. My first night there, they were beginning a book study on <u>Every Man's Battle: Winning The War On Sexual Temptation</u>. I knew that this was where I needed to be. I would go to the study every week, read the book and participate in the discussions, but I never let anyone in on my struggles with lust.

Everything at work was going good. I was doing great at my job, and my employees seemed to love and respect me. I had always been a hard worker since my youth. My father always modeled hard work and being a man of your word. Those principles got me far in life. So the next thing that happened caught me way off guard. I got a call from the owner that he needed to talk to me in his office. This wasn't anything new. He was the one I reported to, so I didn't think anything of it. I walked up to his office and he asked me to take a seat. He said he was having to make some budget cuts and couldn't afford to keep my position any longer.

This had to be a dream. I had never been reprimanded at a job, much less fired! They had made this position for me to be able to come on staff, and business was slower than normal so they couldn't afford to keep me. I worked out my notice and began my job hunt. I felt like God was showing me in that season that He is my provider. He got me the job and He could take it away. I had lost my connection with Him, and that was much more important than my salary.

Shortly after my job loss, the men's group I was attending invited me to a weekend men's retreat in Georgia. I didn't know what to expect, but I didn't have an excuse not to go, so I said yes. I knew that my fire was dying out and I wanted nothing more than to get it back. I was reading more and praying more, but I still felt distant from God. That weekend away was going to be exactly what I needed, I just knew it.

I arrived at the retreat to find men from all walks of life, of all ages, who had this special bond in Christ. Men with a genuine love for one another, taking their masks off and sharing their struggles. Men confiding in each other, encouraging one another and showing true brotherly love. This was the first time I had ever seen men being that transparent and real, and it changed my life.

I walked into that weekend with a lot of secret struggles that I had never opened up to anyone about. I remember a part of the weekend where we got to share our testimony with our group. This was my chance to get it all off of my shoulders, I was pumped! I went through my whole testimony, but I left out anything to do with lust and pornography. I was kicking myself the rest of the day. That night, I tracked down a guy who had a similar story to my own and made him listen to the whole thing. That was the first time that I ever shared the whole truth to anyone. It was freeing and I felt as though the barrier was gone. My fire was re-ignited and I was on top of the world.

You see, I saw my first porn magazine when I was 9 years old. From there, things escalated to chat rooms and exchanging fake pictures with female strangers on the internet at the young age of 11. By the time I was in middle school, my addiction to this lust drug was out of control. It changed the way I viewed women and it changed the way I looked at life. Girls were no longer humans to love and cherish, but objects to be used for my pleasure. I didn't battle the addiction until a lot later in life, and by then it seemed unbeatable. That was something so secret and so shameful that no one ever knew. In my eyes, no one needed to know. It was my struggle and I wanted to keep it that way. However, the freedom I found by confessing it was amazing.

It took almost a year after that for me to confess it to my wife. I had a deep fear of how she would react. I just knew that she wouldn't be able to forgive me. Fear is crippling, and usually it's for no reason. That fear was the only thing standing between me and true freedom. I couldn't carry around the guilt of this un-confessed sin any longer. I began to ask for God to prepare her heart and give me an opening. He gave me an opening alright! We were laying in bed one night and she asked me out of nowhere, *"What are the things that you struggle with?"* It was a clear opening, yet I dodged the question like anytime in the past. I told her of some alcohol, drugs, and cigarette addictions that I had battled. She got up and walked towards the bathroom. Then she looked back at me and asked, *"Thats all? Are you sure?"* I spilled the beans to her only to find out that she had known all along. She said that she knew what a heart I had for men that struggled with that and she figured that it must have been something personal to me. What a relief it brought to have that out in the open!

After sharing my testimony with the man at the retreat, I met a guy there from California who had brought about 30 men with him. They did this chant that I couldn't get out of my head. He would come into a room and just yell at the top of his lungs, "JESUS!" Then all of the guys would yell, "FREES US!" It shook the room and brought something to life in all the men. I asked him later what the chant was all about and he told me that it was their battle cry. He went on to tell me about the 300+ men from back home who were soldiers of Christ. He looked me in the eye and said, *"You ever asked a marine if he's in the marines? He stands up real tall and sticks his chest out and says 'Ya, I'm a Marine!' He's proud of it! Well that's how all my guys are about Jesus. They are proud to claim the name of Christ and they won't back down for nothing!"*

Coming back home, I realized I desperately needed to have a community of brothers to do life with like that every week. I did not intend on having some large group. I just wanted to meet with a guy or two every week and keep the mask off. I started meeting with a couple of men and since then the group has blown up. I didn't realize what a need there was for other men to experience the kind of freedom that this brought. There's something about looking another man in the eyes and confessing your sins to him that's powerful. It brings healing. It is true that in 1 John 1:9 we are told, *"If we confess our sins, then He is faithful and just to forgive us our sins and to cleanse us from all unrighteousness."* But if confessing privately to God was all that was needed, then why did the Holy Spirit have James instruct us to confess our sins one to another? To have nothing hidden in the darkness removes a very heavy weight that was never intended for us to carry in the first place.

Now I want to emphasize something here. Being vulnerable is not the end, but the door-way into something much greater. There must be a deeper "why" to our opening up beyond just getting the weight off of our shoulders. The purpose to removing the mask cannot be only so that it gets easier to share our struggles and then we continue on in those struggles. By taking the mask off and being completely vulnerable in our brokenness to others, it allows us to receive Christ's love through them. The mask we wear serves as a barrier to receiving that love. As long as we have this front up, it is not us who receives the love, but actually the false version of ourselves. This feels good in the moment, but is completely superficial. When we take the mask off and allow even the worst of ourselves to be seen, it provides a way for God to penetrate and transform like never before.

Since starting the group, we have multiplied several times and have "Jesus Frees Us" groups at a couple different churches as well as in several homes. Many men have started groups modeled after the one I lead. There is a morning group for people in real estate that a broker friend of mine started in order to reach the guys in his industry. Two of the men in my group lead one on another night for guys that are fresh out of jail. Also, my wife and her best friend started a group similar to ours for women.

Pretty soon, we will be launching several more groups all at once. We are putting together a weekend event with campfires, games, speakers and discussion times. All the men in the current groups that are ready to lead their own will head up one of the smaller circles. It is my hope that by the end of the weekend they will have started deep relationships with the men at their tables and have the ability to continue weekly meetings with them after it's over. These groups extend far beyond our weekly meetings. These men have become my family. We keep up with each other throughout the week with encouraging messages or thought provoking questions that make us dig deeper into Scripture. A lot of us go to church service together on the weekends and out to dinner afterwards with our families. We plan outings together for special occasions. We serve together and we live as the church to the best of our abilities as described in the book of Acts.

Having a community of believers that I can be transparent with week after week has been a huge weapon in my fight against temptation. If you have been wearing a mask your whole life, then it doesn't have to stay that way. Take it off today and let the world see the real you.

Be You

Jesus frees us from needing the approval of others. Winston Churchill once said, *"When you're 20, you care what everyone thinks, when you're 40 you stop caring what everyone thinks, when you're 60, you realize no one was ever thinking about you in the first place."* Why do we waste so much time trying to fit into the mold of other people's perception and ignoring the One whose thoughts of us truly matters? Jesus frees us from being someone we're not. He frees us to live for an audience of One. Make a decision every morning that God's approval is the only one you need and live like it day in and day out.

Jesus Frees Us

"Fill your mind with God's Word and you will have no room for Satan's lies."

Unknown

4

Renew Your Mind

"Do not conform to this age, but be transformed by the renewing of your mind, so that you may discern what is the good, pleasing and perfect will of God."
Romans 12:2

If you really are this new creation, if old things are truly passed away and if all things have actually became new, then why do you keep thinking the same way and struggling with the same things? I'm going to let you in on a little secret... You still haven't fully renewed your mind!

This may come as a shocker to you, but when you are born again you are a new creation in your spirit. You still have the same flesh and bones that can still get sick, bleed, break and die. The same mind that can choose to look with lust or cuss like a sailor can also sing praises to God. Your spirit is what has been made new. God has given you a new spirit born of His Spirit. With your new spirit, God has put His desires in your heart as well. The difficulty is in getting those desires from your heart to your head. That's where renewing your mind comes into play.

Persistence Is Key

When you plant a new garden, you have to be on a strict schedule of watering the seeds for a long period of time before you see any growth. It is the same way with your spiritual walk and the renewing of your mind with the truth of God's Word. You have to consistently and routinely water the seed of God's Word, and implant it into your mind over and over again until you begin to see the fruit burst forth in your life. Also, in the same way that a new plant can die quickly from a scorching heat before it has any serious root growth, the Word that you're implanting in your mind can be snatched away by the trials of this life prior to you being rooted and grounded in your faith.

We have been living for the world and listening to the lies for our entire life up to the point that God saved our souls. Renewing your mind from it's old way of thinking doesn't happen overnight. The more we saturate our minds with God's truth, the easier it becomes to recognize the lie. My pastor has a close friend that is in the secret service. He went to visit him at his office one day. When he walked up to his cubical he saw a large stack of counterfeit 100 dollar bills sitting on his desk. The agent told him to pick it up and look through them. Looking closely through the stack my pastor said, *These look so real! How can you tell the difference?"* His friend responded, *"The only way you can recognize a fake is from handling the real thing over and over and over again."* That's it!!! If we want to recognize the truth from the lie and not be deceived, we have to spend a lot of time with and get to know the real thing (Jesus and the Word of God).

In my men's group there is a common theme when people start slipping back into their old ways or losing the battle with temptation. It is almost always directly correlated with time away from reading the Bible. We always seem to do much better when spending time in God's Word. It's not even that the things that cause us to stumble change, but on the inside we are more at peace and better equipped to handle whatever comes our way. It's because we are saturating our minds with the truth and spending time with Jesus. So when the lie and temptation pops up, we can much more easily just brush it aside. It's when we aren't in the Word and we begin to mull over tempting thoughts that we begin to give in to that temptation. If we can capture the thoughts that go against what God says and replace them with the truth found in His Word, then we can overcome.

Live It Out

"But be doers of the word, and not hearers only, deceiving yourselves."
James 1:22

Once we establish a routine of spending time reading the Word, we need to cultivate a discipline of applying it to our lives. Small steps of obedience unleash the power of God. It's not that we have to make these huge leaps of faith, but as we step by step align our lives to the teachings of Scripture, God transforms us. He's not interested in us adding Him to our list of priorities and making minor adjustments here and there. He wants to turn our lives completely upside down. That might sound a bit scary to you, but as we slowly see Him moving in our life, we become more and more open to a complete overhaul.

Free will means that we must be intentional about handing over the reins to God. We have the free will to deny God or submit to Him, and we can change our mind day by day and moment by moment. We must make the decision each and every day, multiple times a day, to deny ourselves and follow Him. That is what it means to be a disciple of Christ. Jesus said, *"If anyone wants to follow after me, let him deny himself, take up his cross daily and follow me." Luke 9:23.* This concept of denying ourselves goes against everything that we have ever known. We live a life of self seeking and selfishness from birth. To deny ourselves is to let go of all one is or ever hopes to be. To let go of all that one has or ever hopes to have. To release all personal rights to oneself, all personal aspirations and all aspects of one's life. To deny yourself in the pursuit of following Christ is to leave behind the attempt to be your own master. To empty your hands of the illusion of control and hand it over into the safe keeping of the only one with true control, our Heavenly Father. Simply put, if you are living for yourself, you're not following Jesus!

Something I have found to ring true in my walk and in the lives of many others is this: Between the conception of our spiritual birth and our first big trial, God gives us enough of Himself and tangible moments of His power worked out through our life to keep us coming back. Between the moment I gave my life to follow Christ and when my fire started going out, I had enough times of seeing God move in, through, and all around me to know that He was real. When you feel God's anointing in your life and then you lose it, it doesn't go unnoticed. It's in that moment that you want nothing more than to have that touch from God back. To know He's with you and to feel His power.

Why Am I Here?

Let me tell you the story of David. Not David in the Bible, but the David in my group. David was a friend of a friend that I hung out with a few times several years prior to him reaching out to me. He messaged me over Facebook late one night asking what kind of Bible I read. This was very random, so I started to pry. He ended up telling me that he had been battling drugs and alcohol to mask his anxiety and depression most of his life. We messaged back and forth for a while and he ended up saying his life lacked purpose. Now if you saw this guy from the outside, you would never know these things. He had a beautiful wife that had been by his side since grade school and now he was 37 years old. He had 2 kids, another on the way, a nice house, nice cars and a great job. All of these things that we classify as success or the *American Dream*, yet he felt empty.

I told him that I was going to pick him up on Wednesday night and bring him to my small group. I started to drag him along for several weeks. I knew if he didn't ride with me he probably wouldn't come. Week after week on the ride home from group, I would miss his exit because of the deep conversations we were in. The group purchased him his first Bible and began to pray over him a lot. He was not a believer in Christ, but he was hoping there was something to all of this Jesus stuff he heard us talk about. Through several months of him reading the Bible, praying and seeing God move in the men's lives at group week after week, he was determined that this was everything he was searching for. One issue still remained. He wasn't ready to give up his old way of life. He wasn't ready to truly surrender.

During the weeks that preceded, he began to read his Bible everyday and pray. He would stop himself at times when doubts crept into his mind and wonder, *"Who am I even praying to? Do I even really believe all this?"* Then he would have weeks that he would say, *"I'm never going to be the same! I have this peace that I've never had in my life and it's all from God!"* So while God was giving David a taste of His presence, it wouldn't last. David still wasn't ready to get off of the fence and come over to Jesus' side completely. He felt like something still had to happen for him to fully submit. He told me that he had laid down for people his whole life, but for some reason he wasn't going to budge when it came to this. He said, *"If I say I accept Christ, it's going to be real and all in!"*

David's boss at work was a Christian and started to talk to David about God as well. One day he called him into his office. He spent hours trying to lead him to salvation only for David to come to the gate and refuse to go in. That afternoon David called me to tell me all about it. He said, *"I don't want to be just another notch in my boss' belt. Plus, something still just isn't clicking and I don't know what it is."* I recalled a story from my old pastor about a lady who was spiritually blinded to the truth because of a demonic attachment to her. It had to do with her previous involvement with the occult. I also shared the parable of the seeds and the different soils with him and told him I thought he was the rocky ground and the stone under the surface needed to be removed. I said that I would be praying for his spiritual eyes to be opened to God's truth and the stone to be removed. He texted me the next day and asked if I prayed that prayer. That was right after I finished praying for him the second time that day. He told me that he just read Romans 2:4 and it hit him like a ton of bricks.

"Or do you despise the riches of His kindness, restraint, and patience, not recognizing that God's kindness is intended to lead you to repentance?"
Romans 2:4

David thought that he was the one doing all the work and chasing after God all these months, then suddenly he realized it was the other way around. This whole time God was actually pursuing him. David got called back into his boss's office right after reading that scripture. During their time together, his boss told him that he didn't need another notch in his belt and discussed the parable of the seeds with him. These were the exact things David and I talked about the night before. David gave his life to Christ that day and left his old ways behind.

After accepting Christ and committing to following Him, David immediately had this heavy weight come down on his shoulders. He thought about what he just did and wondered if he could live up to it. He walked into his office and sat down in front of his computer. As he looked at the screen saver of a mountain range with the sun peaking through, something happened. The sun began to shine very brightly and he heard an audible voice say, *"He loves you."* Immediately after hearing that voice, the heavy weight was lifted. David began to find joy and contentment in reading God's Word and sharing his testimony to help others. He would still have times of anxiety, but he no longer coped through drugs and alcohol. Now he could run to Jesus in those times and find true peace from the Prince of Peace.

Who Moved?

About a year into his walk, David had a small relapse. He had fallen back into some of his old ways. He came to group and confessed everything to the men there. Then he went on to say, *"I know that what happened to me was real. It wasn't something I made up in my head. There's so many times and situations I can look back on where I saw God moving in my life. I've gotta get back in the Word and back to living my life for Jesus."*

He went through an extremely stressful season that got him off course and pulled his focus off of Christ. However, as he began to look back at the times where God showed up, and as he could feel that lost connection that he once had with Jesus, he wanted nothing more than to get it back. Then, right there in group he repented of his sins and dedicated himself back to seeking God wholeheartedly. The next week I saw him and his whole countenance had changed. He had that fire back and it was evident. David said one day, *"Anytime I slip, God is right there waiting to take me by the hand. If I ever feel like God is distant, I know it's me that moved and not Him."* Over the course of his first year walking with Jesus and other Christians, reading the Bible and praying, his mind was slowly being renewed. It is a process, but the reward far outweighs the work you put in. David now leads his own "Jesus Frees Us" group on Friday nights.

"For our momentary light affliction is producing for us an absolutely incomparable eternal weight of glory."
2 Corinthians 4:17

God Lens

There are a number of ways that we can go about renewing our mind. The main objective in doing so would be to get our eyes on Jesus and see things from His perspective versus a worldly perspective. Our natural inclination is to view things from the world's perspective. That's just how we were raised and thats how we were taught. Even if we grew up in a Christian home, we still grew up with the world, peers, media, etc. influencing the way we look at things. So basically, anything that we can use to concentrate our focus on Jesus and change our way of thinking to an eternal perspective is renewing our mind. Romans 12:2 tells us the purpose of renewing our minds is to be transformed and to know the will of God.

As our minds are renewed over time, we begin to look at things differently. The way we view the world, the way we view our purpose and value, and the way we see trials and tribulations when they come are now different. They begin to be seen through a God lens and from an eternal perspective. Everything is put in it's place as being light and momentary in the grand scheme of eternity. How much would this world change if we could just see people and circumstances through God's eyes? Renewing our minds through the continuous reading and applying of Scripture to our lives does just that!

Developing An Appetite For God

To hunger and thirst for God is completely upside down and backwards from physical hunger. The longer we go without eating food, the hungrier we get. Then we eat a big meal and we are full and satisfied *(we don't want anymore)*. Not so with spiritual hunger. The longer we go without feeding on the Word of God, the less hungry for godliness we are. On the other hand, the more we feed on the Word, the hungrier we get. If you find yourself not being hungry for God's Word or having a desire to spend time with Him, I encourage you to force feed yourself. As you do this more and more, the hunger will continue to grow.

So now what? How can you begin to cultivate this habit of renewing your mind? Start by making a decision to read the Word daily. Start a Bible reading plan and stick to it. Get in a group that will hold you accountable to staying on course and challenge you to live out what you read. You may be thinking, *"Great... Another list."* But, I seriously can't emphasize enough how important true community is to your spiritual formation and growth. You cannot do this alone!

Jesus frees us from our sinful flesh so that it may not rule over us any longer. Instead, we who are in Christ are dead to sin and alive to God. The truth of His Word transforms us as we begin to believe it and stand firm in it. His life rules over our bodies and our minds so that we are a weapon used for His righteousness.

"For we know that our old self was crucified with him so that the body ruled by sin might be rendered powerless so that we may no longer be enslaved to sin, since a person who has died is freed from sin."
Romans 6:6,7

Jesus Frees Us

"To be a missionary you don't have to cross the sea, you just have to see the cross."

Mark Cahill

5

Divine Appointments

"A person's heart plans his way, but the LORD determines his steps." Proverbs 16:9

Have you ever heard of "Divine Appointments"? I classify a *divine appointment* as a situation where God makes an open door with somebody in your day to day activities that gives you the opportunity to share and glorify Jesus. Whether that be to encourage another believer in their walk with Christ to be more bold, or to introduce a non-believer to the person of Jesus for the very first time. Maybe it's someone who doesn't believe or is unsure because they have never experienced God or met a Christian who is genuine and authentic in their relationship with Jesus. Or maybe it's someone who considers themselves a Christian simply because of some prayer they prayed a long time ago, but they never actually decided to *follow* Jesus. There are a number of ways that a divine appointment can play out, but it is always marked by God being glorified in some way.

The Great Commission

The great commission is to "Go into all the world and preach the gospel." The gospel means the "good news" of Jesus. If we aren't sharing Jesus with the world around us, then can we really call ourselves followers of Christ? Jesus said, *"All authority in heaven and on earth has been given to me, therefore GO!!!"* This is something that we ought to take quite seriously. We don't want to be commanded to make disciples and show up to heaven empty handed, never to have made one disciple. How serious do we take the commands of the one we call Lord if we are not willing to get out of our comfort zone to obey him?

"Why do you call me, 'Lord, Lord,' and don't do the things I say?" Luke 6:46

Get Uncomfortable

Being an introvert, it is never easy for me to speak to strangers about anything, much less a confrontational topic such as Jesus. However, if I am serious about being a true follower of Christ, then I am going to have to learn to get uncomfortable. It's been a long process and it still isn't easy, but I intentionally go about everyday looking for opportunities to share Jesus with those around me. Sometimes that includes sharing what Jesus has done in my life, sometimes it means praying with someone that's going through a difficult time and sometimes that means listening to what someone else believes in order to combat the lies and show them the truth of God's Word. The more often we do this, the more comfortable it gets.

Something that I do every morning is pray for God to order my steps and create opportunities for me to share Jesus with others. I also pray that God gives me the courage and boldness to step into those opportunities when they happen. Since I pray for divine appointments everyday, when the opportunity presents itself, I am not caught off guard. I am intentionally looking for them in every conversation that I have. When you live intentionally everyday for Christ, it is the most rewarding and exciting life that you can live. People think that becoming a Christian means becoming boring. That couldn't be farther from the truth. If you live your life intentionally following Jesus and seeking to obey everything that He commands us in Scripture, there is no other way of living that can even compare. It's not about following a bunch of rules. It's about letting God transform your life, so that you can be an instrument He uses everywhere you go. It's about abiding so close in Jesus, that you begin to look and talk like Him to the world around you. When we allow God's Word and His Holy Spirit to guide our life, the adventure never ends.

I inspect homes for a living. When I go to inspect a house, the buyer of that home is my client-not the homeowner. I rarely even meet the owner of the home because their agent advises them to not be there at the time of the inspection. Well this day, I pulled up to my inspection and the homeowner came out of the front door in somewhat of a panic and started apologizing for being there. She told me on the verge of tears that the home she was trying to buy was falling through and she had no other place to go. She said that there was a lot wrong with this house and she had no money to fix it. She went on to explain that the buyers have already mentioned several things they wanted fixed prior to closing.

I did my best to comfort her quickly and get on with the reason I was there. I told her it was her house, and it was fine that she was there. She went inside, and I went on with my job. When I entered the home, she was sitting in the living room and seemed to have calmed down quite a bit. We made small talk as I inspected the rooms around where she was sitting. Up to this point, I had just felt sorry for her and wanted her to be comforted and at peace. I didn't realize that God may have put her directly in my path that day to share the Prince of Peace (Jesus) and His Comforter (Holy Spirit) with her.

When I got finished and was about to leave, I

felt a nudge to offer to pray with her. I walked up to the door from my truck and rang the door bell. She opened the door and I told her I was all finished. She said, *"Okay, well it was nice to meet you. You have a good rest of your day."* I asked her if she minded if I pray with her over everything she was going through. Her eyes got wide and she responded, *"I would love that!"*. I stepped towards her, took her hands and bowed my head. I prayed for God to reveal Himself to her in a mighty way. For Him to send His Holy Spirit to comfort her in her time of need. For her to know His Son, the Prince of Peace from whom all peace comes. For God to meet her needs and help all that she was facing to miraculously work out. After I had finished praying I opened my eyes to see tears streaming down her cheeks. I told her to have a blessed day and left.

I didn't think a whole lot about it until a couple weeks later. My boss calls me to tell me he just got off the phone with a sellers agent who I inspected a home for a couple weeks ago. He said, *"You prayed with her client that was there, do you remember her?"* I said yes... I didn't know what was coming next. Did she call to complain? I really had no clue. He then went on to tell me that the lady I prayed for had told her agent prior to that appointment that she didn't know how to talk to God and didn't really know what a relationship with Jesus or a prayer life looked like. Through my one simple prayer with her, she has begun a prayer life of her own, and was now seeking a relationship with God. *"What you did that day could have changed this womans life!"*, my boss told me. He then went on to say that even though that house had a ton of things wrong with it, the buyers ended up not asking for much to be done and didn't even request for the original items they had mentioned before the inspection. *"That's a God thing right there!"* said my boss.

The way I prayed isn't what's important. The things I said to her aren't what matters. The fact that I felt a nudge from God and obeyed is what made the difference. When God asks you to move, do you move? Or do you brush it off and go about your day because life's busy. God wants to use you wherever you are. He doesn't need you to be an eloquent speaker, able to quote Scripture, able to pray earth shattering prayers, or any other excuse we come up with. He only needs you to be available.

Take Church To Them

Often, we as Christians rely on our pastor to teach us about God and to convert our friends. We invite friends to our church to hear the gospel preached instead of being the church and bringing the gospel to them. It's not wrong to invite people to church, but that can't be the only way they hear about Jesus. Church as we know it is to be the weekly assembly of believers. But we are the church, and we are not confined to a building. We as believers are to take Jesus with us and display Him to the world around us.

We walk past lost people everyday and don't

even look twice. People that this world sees as trash. A lot of things the world calls trash, Jesus calls treasure. A lot of times we have people that we just don't want to be around because it's uncomfortable. We need to get uncomfortable and depend more upon God and less upon ourselves. It doesn't take a man or woman of God to point out the trash in somebody's life. But it takes a man or woman of God to pull the treasures out of what the world calls trash. It's time to be radical. What are we doing with the gospel? It's time that you reach down deep and grab hold of the blood of Jesus and realize you are a Son or a Daughter of God. You were made for so much more than what you're living out! Be bold!!!

When Things Don't Go As Planned

Sometimes it's very evident that we are in a divine appointment. Unexplainable connections are made and everything just seems to click. We find ourselves baffled at how God worked this out. Other times it's not so evident. We feel the nudge and know it's from God. We start to move in and things don't go as planned. Maybe we are met with hostility or the person just doesn't seem interested. If you felt the nudge, then keep pressing forward. Don't let the way things appear to push you off course. We walk by faith, not by sight. There could be a lot going on behind the scenes that you just can't see happening at the time. The majority of the time when we plant a seed, we may not see what comes of that seed. One plants, one waters, but it is God who brings the increase.

An example of this is a divine appointment that I had several months ago. I was on my way to a morning inspection and praying for an opening to share Jesus with someone. Before I pulled up to the house, I had a strong feeling that the real estate agent at that inspection was supposed to be my divine appointment. When I got there, the buyer's agent named Matt walked up to my truck. Within the first minute of us talking, several curse words came out of his mouth. He wasn't mad, he was actually quite upbeat. However, from the language he was using I started strongly questioning if the nudge I felt was accurate. I found some common ground through a mutual friend who was an agent on his team. I shared with him how I met the friend a few months back, which was at an inspection where I shared Jesus with him. Since then, me and the guy had met for breakfast a couple times. I used the relationship I had cultivated with our mutual friend to transition into talking to Matt about God.

Through the whole conversation, it felt like a dead end. He was polite and listened, but you could tell that he wasn't really interested. I told him about my mens group and invited him to come check it out sometime. He thanked me for the invite and we ended up parting ways. I got in the truck thanking God for the seeds that were sown. Whether it goes good or bad, I always get joy out of witnessing. I know that even if the person didn't like what I said, it still pleased God. Several weeks went by, and I got a message from Matt on Facebook. His son had a head on head collision in a football game and went limp on the field. He told me they were in the emergency room and things weren't looking good. He asked for prayer, so I sent the request out to every prayer warrior I could think of. Things turned around for the good. His son went home the next day with a severe concussion. I stayed in contact with him on and off to keep updated on his boy. His son got released by his doctors and I didn't hear from him anymore.

About a month later, I was standing in line at the DMV. I got there early and was the fourth person in line. When I got to the counter and received my paperwork, I looked over to see Matt sitting in the waiting area. I approached him, and said ,*"What's up man? How have you and your family been?"* He looked at me and said, *"Take a seat and I'll tell you."* I sat down next to him and he proceeded to pour out his soul to me through tears for the next 20 minutes. They called my number several times and then passed me, but I knew I couldn't get up from this conversation. He told me that his wife had left him a few days ago and he never even saw it coming. He was in deep depression over losing her and had been having suicidal thoughts. I talked with him for a while and got his phone number. I asked him to come to group that week and we kept in contact until then.

When Matt came into group that week, he started weeping before we even started. He shared what he was going through right out of the gate and could not stop crying. The whole group started pouring into him and showing him love. Since then, this group of men has encouraged Matt to get into

God's Word and lean fully upon Jesus for direction. Several guys would meet up with him one on one and reach out to him with encouragement and advice.

Our group received a message from Matt about a month after he started coming that said, *"I love you all and you have been there for me in my darkest hours and you along with God have not let me down in my struggle. God and you guys have shown me love, mercy, and grace. I now know what it is to have His presence in my life. Thank you!"*

Several months since then, he is still in group and seeking God with his whole heart. His wife and him are now back together and their relationship is better than ever. What before seemed completely lost, God has reunited. Matt is learning to lead his wife and kids towards Jesus. He routinely prays with them and strikes up conversations with strangers in hopes to share God's love. What an amazing testimony of God's faithfulness. He moves mountains that seem absolutely immovable to us. Our God is still in the business of performing miracles.

I now know exactly why God impressed it upon my heart to talk to Matt that day. Nothing in that moment seemed to line up or make sense, but God was working behind the scenes. He knew what was about to happen in this man's life, and He positioned me to be there for him when he needed me. God orchestrated us meeting up a day after his wife left in that waiting room at the DMV. God knew that he would be at the end of his rope and need someone to point him to Jesus.

I could have easily seen how Matt was talking when we first met and ignored God's nudge because it wasn't comfortable or easy. Thankfully, I had already told God that morning that I was going to die to myself and do whatever He wanted me to do. If you have been purchased by the blood of Jesus, then you are not your own, you are His! You have a growing desire in your heart to be used by Him.

Do You Hear His Voice?

Another crazy God moment I want to share with you is one my wife had years ago. Halee and I were driving down the road on our way home. We were less than a mile from our house when we passed a man in an electric scooter sitting on the edge of his driveway. The man seemed to be enjoying the day and was throwing a stick back and forth with his dog. We waved at him and he waved back. We got about a quarter mile down the road and Halee looked at me and told me to turn around. Puzzled, I asked, *"Why?"* She said, *"Turn around, I think that man needs our help."* Confused I said, *"Why would you think that? He was playing with his dog."* She responded, *"I just got this feeling that we are supposed to help him."* I turned the car around and drove back in front of his house. I rolled my window down and asked him if he needed any help. He exclaimed, *"Yes, my wheel rolled off the edge of my driveway and I've been sitting here for hours praying that God would send someone to help me!"* I pulled into his driveway and got out to help him. As soon as I got his scooter unstuck he said, *"Thank you Jesus!"*

We must die to ourselves daily, multiple times a day in order to live for Him. Paul says in 2 Corinthians 4:10, *"We always carry the death of Jesus in our body, so that the life of Jesus may also be displayed in our body."* Paul was saying that we carry around the sentence of death with us all day, everyday. That means that when something not of God comes up and rears it's ugly head, we have to put it to death. Anything that is not of Jesus, we have to take the knife out and slay it. The second part of that verse is so powerful. It gives us the reason that we must have this daily dying to self. It says we carry around this death of Jesus **so that**... So that the life of Jesus might be made manifest, or displayed in our mortal bodies. If we want to manifest Jesus to others, we have got to die to self and live intentionally for Him.

Jesus Frees Us

"He wants all or nothing. The thought of a person calling himself a Christian without being a devoted follower of Christ is absurd."
Francis Chan

6

What's It Worth?

*"These have come so that the proven character of your faith-
more valuable than gold, which though perishable, is
refined by fire-may result in praise, glory, and honor at the
revelation of Jesus Christ."*
1 Peter 1:7

What's your faith worth to you? Have you ever
asked yourself that question? Has your faith ever cost
you anything? If your faith hasn't cost you anything,
then it's probably not worth very much either.
Scripture instructs us to examine ourselves to see if
we're in the faith (2 Corinthians 13:5). A lot of times

we don't find out what our faith is truly worth until it gets tested. Many will pass the examination but may fail the test. We will be tested and tried in this life so that our faith in Christ may be refined into pure gold before we step into eternity.

A good friend of mine who is a pastor once told me, *"It's easier to preach a thousand sermons than it is to live one."* In other words, it's easier to talk the talk than it is to walk the walk. One way you can know how much your faith is worth to you is how you live it out. If I were to ask you if you would die for Jesus, most of you reading this book would probably say "Yes" without hesitation. However, you can't really know how you would react in that situation until it presents itself. May I suggest that if you won't live for Him, you probably wouldn't die for Him either. In fact, I might even venture to say that it would be easier to die for Him than to live for Him. To live for Him day in and day out when obstacles and challenges come your way is the true test of your faith.

"Consider it great joy, my brothers and sisters, whenever you experience various trials, because you know that the testing of your faith produces endurance. And let endurance have its full effect, so that you may be mature and complete, lacking nothing"
James 1:2-4

Perspective

When trials come your way and life knocks

you off your feet, how do you react? How do you view your trials? Do you view them from the lens of scripture as opportunities to grow in your faith, or do you view them as inconveniences and try to avoid them at all costs? If the testing of your faith produces perseverance and perseverance character, then why don't we count it all as joy? It's because we rarely step back and look at what we're going through from God's perspective. Perspective is *so* important. We get so wrapped up in how we think things should work out that when things don't go exactly how we imagine them, we get frustrated and lose our cool. You can learn a lot about yourself by how you react to circumstances that you weren't expecting.

In the corporate world, there are positions that require you to focus on the big picture of the business. You don't get too involved in the small details. These people are CEO's, executives, directors, etc. Then you have people who still don't get too close, but they manage more of the details than the higher positions. These are positions of management. You have positions at every level all the way down to people in production and quality control. These positions look at all the details and never step back to view the big picture of the business because it's just not their job. Often times, we can't see the forest for the trees. We have to look at things from a certain distance, or through someone else's eyes before we can appreciate their true value. So if you're having trouble and can't seem to focus on God because of all the chaos going on all around you--it's probably time to step back and view things from an eternal or big picture perspective.

As we persevere through various trials and grow in our faith, our character begins to reflect more of the character of Jesus. This life is not all about us, it's about Him. If we can keep our focus on abiding in Jesus and our character reflecting His character, then the tests and trials we go through can begin to have purpose. Suddenly we aren't viewing our circumstances from such a close up view, but from how God can use them to shape and mold us into who we were created to be. We were created to be a people in perfect communion with our Creator, and who reflect His love, character, and values like a mirror to the world around them.

God doesn't want a stagnant relationship with us. If we are not growing closer to God then we are, in fact, growing further away. It's like a bicycle. You must be moving or you will fall down. To remain in the same mental and spiritual condition over long periods of time grieves the Spirit of God who longs to instruct us and mature us in our Christian life. He does that as we continually look to Him and His Word for guidance through whatever obstacles come our way.

His Yoke and His Burden

"Come to Me, all you who are weary and burdened, and I will give you rest. Take up My yoke and learn from Me, because I am lowly and humble in heart, and you will find rest for your souls. For My yoke is easy and My burden is light."
Matthew 11:28-30

This is Jesus speaking. So what does this really mean for us? What is He trying to tell us? Obviously He is speaking to those at their wits end who are carrying burdens that their shoulders cannot support. Those who are tired and who don't see how they can even go on.

Then He speaks of this yoke of His. He says to take His yoke upon you and learn from Him, and then you will find rest for your souls. So what is this yoke? A yoke is a wooden beam or fitted piece of wood that pair two oxen together to share the load of what they are pulling. Jesus says take His yoke and learn from Him. Obviously He is offering to help us carry the weight of life's burdens here. But when you yoke two animals together, they must go the same direction or they will struggle to do anything. They are yoked together to where they must work in unison. When we take His yoke we are not putting Jesus under our yoke but putting ourselves under His. He says learn from Him. We must agree to walk along side Him or we can do nothing. As we walk with Him, He helps us bear the weight of all we are carrying.

Jesus goes on to tell us His yoke is easy and His burden is light. We must remember that we are put under His yoke and not our own. There are a couple reasons why His yoke is easy and His burden is light. First of all His yoke is easy because we don't have to be the captain of our own ship anymore. We only have to follow Him to whom we're yoked. He is leading the way, we just have to walk with Him. His burden is light because the outcomes are no longer up to us! Our responsibility is to let Him lead, to do what He says in His Word, and to leave the rest up to Him.

Just like in a family we want our children to follow God. That is a deep desire that we should have, but it cannot be our goal. If we make it our goal, then we will view the success of our parenting in whether or not they do what we envision them doing in the way that we envision them doing it. If we have goals for them to be a Christian doctor in Uganda and they decide to be a lead guitarist in a rock band, we feel as though we are failures. When you base your sense of self worth on the success of your own personal plans, your life becomes a long, emotional roller-coaster ride. Instead, our goal as a parent is to become the father or mother that God desires for us to be. We do what He puts on our heart and what He says in His Word, and we leave everything else up to Him. It takes the pressure off of us. So Jesus' yoke is easy and His burden is light because the outcomes are all up to Him. We are simply called to walk in faith and follow Him.

We as a people are so used to micromanaging and controlling the outcomes in everything we do. We think that our way is the best way and if things aren't done to our standards then they must be wrong. Therefore, we want to control every situation, every dollar, every action, everything to do with our kids or marriage, and everything that may impact our future.

This desire to control everything causes a lot of

stress and anxiety. The thing is, we don't have any real control, we just think we do. The more we walk according to the Spirit and the less we walk according to the flesh, the more we begin to realize this truth. When we become free from the sense of having to control everything, we are free to walk in His ways and not our own. This is great news! Jesus frees us from the burden of outcomes. When we are free in Jesus, we are free to walk by faith and let the chips fall where they may.

Praying With A Psychic

My friend Darren is a plumber by trade. He recently had a plumbing job at a palm reading business. He was not too happy about going there, but knew that God is stronger than any demonic force that may be in that house. When he arrived at the job, an elderly lady answered the door. She took him to the bathroom where a clogged toilet was. As he looked around the bathroom he noticed several holes punched in the drywall and sections of the drywall had been ripped off the walls. The lady told him that her grandson is on dope and evidently clogged the toilet up with bloody paper towels from shooting up. Darren had his brother die from a heroin overdose a couple years prior. He shared his story with the lady and started witnessing to her about Jesus. The lady had statues of Jesus and Mary throughout the home as well as strange altars of worship. She was saying some strange prayers in the background while Darren was working on the toilet.

When asked about her beliefs, she told him that she was a Christian and loved the Lord. Darren asked her what about the psychic stuff then. She dodged the question. She then proceeded to tell him that she just wanted to die and she kept saying it over and over. He sat down next to her on the couch and grabbed her hand. He told her that he would be praying for her and for her to have peace. He left after the job was done and went home for lunch. While at home, Darren spent time praying for this lady. He felt a strong pull from God that he was supposed to go back to that house. It was not a comfortable thing to do, but he knew this was Spirit-lead.

Upon arrival, he rang the door bell and the lady opened the door. She invited him in and asked him if he would like a palm reading. He looked her in the eye and said, *"No ma'am, the Holy Spirit told me I needed to come back here and pray with you."* He took her hands and started praying. As he was praying she began to say out loud, *"Lord, I want to die! I just want to die!"* He prayed for the Lord to release her from this demonic spirit that was telling her she wanted to die and to reveal to her how precious life was. He prayed for her to get right with God while she still had time. Then he prayed for her grandson who destroyed her house to be released from the bondage of drug addiction. He quoted scripture saying Jesus is the Way the Truth and the Life. He told her to not give up hope and to turn to Jesus.

After praying, he opened his eyes to her sobbing with tears pouring down her face. She told him, *"Thank you for blessing me, I really needed this."* She told him to come back anytime. The effects of the seed that was planted by Darren's boldness that day may never be known this side of heaven. We do know however that *"God's Word never returns void, but accomplishes what He pleases and will prosper in the thing to which He sent it." Isaiah 55:11*. The outcome of whether she repents and turns to Jesus is not up to Darren. That weight lies with God. Darren's responsibility was to do what God laid on his heart, and that is exactly what he did.

Don't Ignore The Nudges

Have you ever been in such a close relationship where you can feel God's presence and hear His still small voice all the time? You feel him nudging you and you react to it and see Him move? Then the nudges get more difficult and more uncomfortable. Maybe you brush it off as just something in your head. Before long, that still small voice starts fading away to where you can't hear Him speaking anymore. You don't get the nudges that you used to get. That is called quenching the Spirit. As we ignore the nudges and don't listen to the Holy Spirit's promptings, He gets quiet. This is not something that we want to experience. We want to be the one saying, *"Here I am Lord, send me!"* We want to feel His anointing upon our lives and see the fruit of His work in and around us. In order to have that, we must listen to Him when He speaks. We must be faithful in the small things and He will give us more to do. This takes obedience and intentionality.

Darren has reached the place of full surrender. That is why he was willing to get out of his comfort zone and let God lead. He isn't living for himself anymore, there's a new authority over his life and that authority is Jesus. Jesus purchased him with His own blood and He purchased you too. Is He worth losing your life for? Jesus says, *"For whoever wants to save his life will lose it, but whoever loses his life because of me will save it." Luke 9:24.*

So count the cost. What's He worth to you really? What's your faith worth? It should be the substance of everything you hope for. Your faith in God shouldn't just be your first priority, but the priority that all other priorities flow from. If Jesus has truly freed you, then you are fully submitted to Him and the value of your faith has a worth more precious than anything you can compare it to. Be a light in this dark world. Be intentional. Be O.C.D for Jesus. Obedient. Committed. Dedicated.

Jesus Frees Us

"True and absolute freedom is only found in the presence of God."
A.W. Tozer

7

Freedom

"So if the Son sets you free, you really will be free."
John 8:36

There are no chains in Heaven! No chains of addiction, no chains of affliction, no chains of sin, no chains of any kind. When Jesus sets you free, you are free indeed! We must stop allowing our life experiences and circumstances to speak louder than the Word of God. We have got to start believing the truth, because the truth will set us free. Jesus is the truth and His Word is truth.

So you're in Christ and you're free. How do

you live in this freedom? How do you keep the bondage of past sins, struggles and unforgiveness from dragging you down again? If you have made Jesus your Lord and Savior, then you have been set free from your bondage to sin and made a slave to righteousness. Your identity no longer lies in who you were *in* Adam, but in who you are *in* Christ. If you have been buried with Christ, you have also been raised with Christ. Since you have been raised with Christ, you now have victory over the sins that used to enslave you.

Living In Freedom

A good first step in living in freedom is nailing down how you see yourself. Where does your identity lie? Do you see yourself as an alcoholic? Do you see yourself as a pervert? Or do you see yourself as a child of God? Everyone who walks this earth will struggle with a flesh problem in one way or another.

Whether you are anxious, depressed, an alcoholic, a drug addict, a porn addict, or whatever it is, your struggle may be different than the next persons. But God's answer is to help you get back into a right relationship with Him. If we can reconcile our relationship with God and deal with all the barriers that we have put up between Him and ourself, then we can be free. If freedom came simply from making an alcoholic not drink, then we wouldn't need Jesus to set us free. You have to see Jesus as the answer, not just abstaining from whatever sin struggle trips you up. Now don't get me wrong, we are called to live holy and righteous lives. But without Jesus, we can live better than anyone in the world and still miss heaven.

The next step to living in the freedom that Christ has purchased for you is to believe that He has called you to be victorious over sin. Christ does not call us to anything that He does not equip us for. You can be sure that God has equipped you if you have a desire to serve Him. God would not put that desire in your heart if He hadn't provided everything you need in order to fulfill it. The problem we have in believing that we can be victorious over sin is that we keep looking back at all the times we've failed.

Instead of sinning, confessing, sinning, confessing, sinning, confessing... We need to confess and follow it up with true *repentance*. Once we have truly repented of our sin (turned from it and walked toward Jesus), we can then enter into the long ongoing process of renewing our mind.

Instead of focusing our mind on not sinning, we are told to fix our eyes on things above, not on things below.(Col. 3:2) Fix your eyes on Jesus, the author and perfecter of your faith.(Heb. 12:2) Whatever is true, whatever is honorable, whatever is pure, whatever is lovely, whatever is praiseworthy, think on those things.(Phil. 4:8) We are never told to focus on not sinning. We stop sinning by keeping our focus on Jesus. Only He can set us free.

Dead To Sin

If we are not tired of our sin and have a true hatred for it, then we probably wont be quick to turn from it. We must come to a place of true repentance where we give our old nature a proper burial. Have you ever told God that you were going to be a living sacrifice for Him, only to crawl right back off the altar soon after? If we are not truly dead to self, then we will not go long without seeking to serve self. We have to make a conscious decision out of our love for God to lay our sin on the altar and kill it. Anything not of Christ, we have got to cut it off.

Have you had your funeral yet? Kyle Idleman wrote: *"Following Jesus isn't about trying everyday, it's about dying everyday."* You want to have true freedom in Christ? You want to really live? To truly live, we must first die. Die to sin and die to self.

What is freedom? If you have free will, then doesn't that mean you're free? No! Whether your struggle is food, or porn, or anger, or whatever else, how do you know if you have freedom from it or not? Can you stop yourself? Can you go without? I'm not asking if you want to stop or if you want to go without, I'm asking can you. To give in to a temptation because you want to and to give in even when you don't want to are two different things. That's what defines freedom from slavery. If I've decided that I am no longer going to drink alcohol because it does nothing life-giving to my marriage, then a week later I say, *"Well one beer or glass of wine wont hurt."*, then I have a problem. If I can't go without it even after recognizing that it does nothing good for me then I am a slave to it.

When we talk about freedom in Christ, we're not talking about being able to do whatever we want. Instead, we are free to delight ourselves in Him. It's about having ourselves chiseled away until we no longer act, behave, or talk like our old self, but like Jesus. It's about this new identity we have in Christ. We don't come to Jesus for justification and then go somewhere else to be sanctified. He promises to be with us and in us through the whole process.

Living In The Light

"This is the judgment: The light has come into the world, and people loved darkness rather than the light because their deeds were evil. For everyone who does evil hates the light and avoids it, so that his deeds may not be exposed."
John 3:19,20

These words from Jesus show us that sin grows and thrives in the darkness, but gets exposed and destroyed in the light. This is much like bacteria, which grows rapidly when left in the dark, but the exposure to light (especially certain kinds of light) kills it. If we want to overcome our sin and walk in the light as He is in the light, then it's time we expose our sin to the light. James 5:16 says,"*Confess your sins to one another and pray for one another so that you may be healed.*" We can't heal what we don't confess. Confessing our sins to the ones we have wronged and others brings that sin into the light where it can be dealt with. *"And Jesus is faithful and just to forgive us of our sins and cleanse us from all unrighteousness." 1 John 1:9.*

It's awkward and uncomfortable to admit our faults to others, but I have found great freedom and accountability in doing so. It's not even that those people are holding me accountable as much as bringing the struggle to light helps me to hold myself accountable. If you want to be free from the bondage of sin, you have to do something aggressive to that sin. You have to expose it to the light. Then, make an accurate assessment of that sin and how it effects you and others. Go through the ramifications of that sin and how awful it truly is to your relationship with God and those around you. Next, make the proclamation to the people you confess to and God that you are never going to do it again. Now, you may be thinking, *"I have said that a million times"*. Well you are probably right, but have you said it out loud to other people and God? Have you done it after humbling yourself to confess the sin to the people you wronged by it? Have you made an accurate assessment of how it effects every aspect of your life? Do all of those things and begin to sit at the feet of Jesus everyday, abiding in Him. Victory WILL come! You are more than a conqueror through Christ Jesus!

I meet people every week who are slaves to something, but they found freedom when they became a slave to Jesus Christ. They were slaves to possessions or slaves to their own pleasures. They were slaves to people and what other people thought about them, but they discovered that true freedom is only found when they live as a slave to Jesus Christ. Instead of shame and bondage and death, we find joy and grace and eternal life. You will never know true freedom until you have completely surrendered and become a slave to Jesus.

Below is a quote from Dietrich Bonhoeffer's book <u>Life Together</u> about the importance of living in the light:

"In confession there takes place a breakthrough to community. Sin wants to be alone with people. It takes them away from the community. The more lonely people become, the more destructive the power of sin over them. The more deeply they become entangled in it, the more unholy is their loneliness. Sin wants to remain unknown. It shuns the light. In the darkness of what is left unsaid sin poisons the whole being of a person. This can happen in the midst of a pious community. In confession the light of the gospel breaks into the darkness and closed isolation of the heart. Sin must be brought into the light. What is unspoken is said openly and confessed. All that is secret and hidden comes to light. It is a hard struggle until the sin crosses one's lips in confession. But God breaks down gates of bronze and cuts through bars of iron (Ps. 107:16). Since the confession of sin is made in the presence of another Christian, the last stronghold of self-justification is abandoned. The sinner surrenders, giving up all evil, giving the sinner's heart to God and finding the forgiveness of all one's sin in the community of Jesus Christ and other Christians. Sin that has been spoken and confessed has lost all of its power. It has been revealed and judged as sin. It

can no longer tear apart the community."

Overcoming Porn

Let me tell you a story about the freedom that I've found in my own struggle against the flesh and how that freedom came about. As I shared with you prior, I have struggled with pornography since a very young age. Let's go a little deeper so that you can begin to grasp the extent of the hold that this sin had on my life. I saw my first porn magazine and tape at the age of 9. By the age of 11, I was watching it on the internet and visiting sex chat rooms. When I got my first cell phone, the addiction escalated to a whole new level.

Relationships with women didn't help the addiction. Instead, they gave it a whole new dimension. I would now watch pornography for the purpose of learning new things to try with my partner. I would even watch porn with my partners as a game of trying to keep up with doing exactly what was on the screen. I now viewed women as an object to be used for my pleasure instead of image bearers of God with value and purpose.

This addiction, like all others gave a short term satisfaction, followed by a long term void that could not be filled. Sex could no longer satisfy and neither could porn. I could have sex three times a day and still need to watch porn to mask the anxiety that it all brought on. Any idle time on my hands would end up being used for self gratification that never truly gratified. I didn't even realize that it was something out of my control until I came to Christ and tried to stop. That's when I found out that I was truly enslaved to my sin struggle.

I began a long process of trying to overcome it in my own strength, all while thinking that I was truly giving it to God. At first, the desire went away. I was so on fire for God that I no longer even thought about it. That lasted until I began to feel the fire go out as I mentioned earlier in the book. As soon as I took my eyes off of God for a second, the desires came back ten fold. I was still going to church, praying a little, reading my bible every now and then and watching porn all at the same time. I knew it was horrible and it made me feel extremely disgusting. Had I lost my salvation? How could I claim to be following Christ, yet at the same time give in to what I knew was pure evil?

This is when I began to really buckle down. I started going to a men's group. I then went to the retreat where I got to confess this struggle for the first time in my life. I felt the weight lifted and felt that I had beat it for good. That lasted a few months and then the temptations came back strong. I began to see that maybe the issue wasn't me being tempted, but my inability to deny my flesh. How could I cut this off for good? What would be my Final "No"?

I would have revelations often that I thought would help me to conquer the temptations. I read in *1 Peter 4:1, "Therefore, since Christ suffered in the flesh, arm yourselves also with the same understanding, because the one who suffers in the flesh is finished with sin."* That was the new thing to help me deny myself. I would pray for God to take these desires away. Then if He didn't, I would suffer through it as Christ suffered through to do the Father's will. That worked great for a time and then I would slip again. I would try to capture the thought when it came and replace it with the truth of God's Word. That would last for a time and then I would slip again. I would make myself confess to my accountability partners every time I sinned. That would last for a time and then I would slip again. I felt as though nothing would be enough to make me deny myself from pornography permanently. I could have months of success, but they always fail at some point when the urges became seemingly too strong.

I was driving down the road one morning on my way to work, thinking about what freedom in Christ meant. Did He really set me free from my slavery to sin? If so, then why hadn't I mastered it yet? I began to wonder what it would take for me to never fall again. Would it take my wife walking in and finding me in the act? Would it take my kids picking up my phone and seeing that filth themselves? Would it take my wife divorcing me out of sheer disgust? I had to figure out what my Final "No" would be, and you have to figure out what yours will be as well.

Maybe the sin that you can't seem to overcome is nothing like mine. Maybe it's a struggle with food.

Maybe it's a struggle with pride. Maybe it's drugs or alcohol. Whatever your struggle is, you've got to master it. God told Cain, *"Sin is crouching at the door; its desire is for you, but you must rule over it."* Genesis 4:7. Christ has brought freedom to your life! He paid for it with His own blood on the cross. But just because He purchased it for you doesn't mean that you don't have a part to play in receiving it.

I can buy my daughter a toothbrush, but unless she puts toothpaste on it and uses it on her teeth the gift is of no benefit. Unless I apply the gift of freedom to my life and my struggles, it is of no benefit to me. God tells me that He has provided me with everything I need for life and godliness.(2 Pt. 1:3) He tells me that when I am tempted, it won't be beyond what I can bear and He will provide a way out.(1 Cor. 10:13) He tells me that I am no longer a slave to sin, but a slave to righteousness.(Rom. 6:18) He tells me that I am now a child of God, holy and redeemed. All these things are true, but we have to apply them to our life. Until our love for God is greater than our love for sin, we will continue to give in to temptation.

So, like I said, my final "No" was mine and you will have to find yours. Before you can determine what yours is, you will first have to come to recognize exactly what your sin does to you. My recommendation would be for you to say out loud or write down all of the pros and cons of your struggle. What do you get out of it good and bad? Short term and long term. What does it do to your relationship with others? What does it do to your relationship with

God? How does it impact your family? How does it impact your wife and your kids? What does it do to your own self-image and worth? Be specific and be honest.

Once you have been able to do that, figure out what kind of force you can put against it. What are some parameters you can put in place? What are some steps you can take that are way more than you want to take? You have to do something drastic to your sin, or else your sin will remain your sin. Once you have applied this overwhelming force against your sin, you are finally ready to give it the Final "No"!

Mine came by way of a promise. Let me give you the back story of this so you can understand why this worked for me. Growing up, my dad was not a spiritual leader. He didn't give me much in that area, but he did teach me many valuable lessons. He taught me to be a hard worker. He taught me how to work with my hands. He taught me to be a man of my word. He ingrained into me that when you tell someone you are going to do something, you do it. He taught me that a promise and my word were such a big deal, that I had to make sure it was truly something I could do before ever bringing it up. He didn't realize it at the time, but he was teaching me something straight out of Scripture. Jesus said, *"Let your yes be yes and your no be no."* In Ecclesiastes 5 it says, *"When you make a vow to God, do not delay to fulfill it. He has no pleasure in fools; fulfill your vow. It is better not to make a vow than to make one and not fulfill it."*

Most people may say that they are a man of their word and a promise means a great deal to them. My question to you is, *"Has it been tested and proven in your life?"* As I was driving to work one morning I recalled something from my past that revealed to me what I had to do. At 17 years old, when I was sitting in jail awaiting my court date, I was praying and asking God to get me out of this mess. I began to promise Him that I would never steal again. I was ready to promise my life away if He would just get me out of this. I was facing up to 15 years in jail as a 17 year old kid. I was desperate! Just as I was about to make these promises, I stopped to count the cost. Could I really hold up my end of the bargain if I commit to these things? I had enough reverence for God to not take what I was saying flippantly. As I sat in that jail cell, I made sure that whatever I promised God, that I would follow through with it.

The big promise that I made was to never steal again. When God came through for me at my court date the way He did, I knew it was time to hold up my end of the deal. That was 15 years ago and I still think about that promise anytime I go to pick something up that doesn't belong to me. I would be in a bank and not take the pen home with me because it was stealing. My word has been tested for the past 15 years of my life, so I know what it's worth to me.

Driving down the road that day, it hit me that I needed to make a promise to God that I would NEVER look at porn again. I had never made that promise before, because I knew my track record. I knew that I was so bad at slipping back into my sin that I would never make such a promise because I don't make promises that I can't keep. In that moment it felt like God whispered to my spirit and said, *"If you promise it, you'll keep it."* I was floored! It was like this light bulb went off and I knew what I had to do.

I was driving down the road, telling God with tears streaming down my face that I would never look at that filth again. I felt the weight of that confession and I trembled as I said it.

Jesus made freedom possible to us, but it is still something that we have to choose. Freedom from our sin does not happen on accident. It is a conscience decision made every day, and some days are easier than others. It is when we think that we are good that we must stand firm or we will fall.(1 Cor. 10:12) It's not that I no longer get tempted by lust, but I refuse to allow myself to be tempted beyond what I can endure. If I feel the temptation coming, I don't entertain it anymore. I have said my Final "No" to that sin in my life and that decision has brought freedom like I've never known. I had to cut that out of my life to be able to closely abide in Christ and bear fruit for His Kingdom. The love and reverence I have for Jesus, combined with a solemn vow made through tears and a daily dying to self is what it takes for me to remain free from the chains of bondage that have enslaved me for the majority of my life. I still have the ability to give in to the flesh if I choose to, but the decision has been made. That decision has to be made every day multiple times a day, but I now have the freedom to make it!

Free Indeed

Jesus frees us from all our chains and bondage. He breaks the barriers that stand between us and freedom. He penetrates every area of our life and sets us free. The addictions that once ruled over our lives cannot stand up to His power over them. The struggles of past hurts, habits, and hang ups must bow down in His presence. He has been given all authority in heaven and on earth, that every knee must bow and every tongue confess that He is Lord! Those knees and those tongues include the things that have stood between you and the person you were created to be as a child of God. Scripture tells us that even the mountains bow down. Start living your life today in the victory that Christ purchased for you some 2000 years ago. His mercies are new every morning. Start fresh today and every day after.

Jesus Frees Us

"True discipleship involves deep relationships. Jesus didn't simply lead a weekly Bible study. He lived life with His disciples and taught through actions as well as words."
Francis Chan

8

Community

"And let us watch out for one another to provoke love and good works, not neglecting to gather together, as some are in the habit of doing, but encouraging each other, and all the more as you see the day approaching."
Hebrews 10:24,25

"I like your Christ, but I do not like your Christians."-Ghandi. Have you ever felt this way? Maybe you still do. Do you see these people that come to church and outwardly claim to be something one day a week that they don't back up with the other 6? Do you see people who wear a "mask" and act like

everything is always great even when it's not? Do you see hypocrites, and it makes you angry? Is it because you see a lot of yourself in them?

Maybe you are actually mad at yourself for putting up this front. Maybe you are beyond that now and just wish the rest of the church would finally get real. Might I suggest that they probably need you to show them what that looks like?

Be Authentic

The majority of people have grown up their whole life never seeing what true community is. Never experiencing anything like what the Bible says Christian community should look like. It's supposed to be a family. If we are in Christ then we have all been adopted as sons and daughters into the family of God. However, the majority of Christians go to church on the weekend and sit next to a bunch of strangers they never talk to. They never take the time to get to know anything about the next person's life, family, interests, struggles, job, etc.

Jesus said the world would know we are His by our love for one another. Is that something you've ever been recognized by? Is it something you've ever seen modeled in your church? Genuine love for your brothers and sisters in Christ. If not, then there may be a disconnect somewhere. Maybe it's time that you get intentional in cultivating real relationships with those you sit next to on Sundays.

I grew up with several friends that were in gangs. The Crips and the Bloods were the thing where I came from. When you joined a gang, you were brought into the family of that gang. They offered you protection from outsiders. If you had an issue, they made it their issue. They were committed to their gang and would even sacrifice their freedom or their lives for the gang in some instances. If someone left that life and came into your church, would they feel like they joined another family or would they feel all alone?

Now I'm not saying that we should be like street gangs, but maybe they have a better grasp on commitment, devotion and family than much of the church today. Obviously they have a lot of errors in the way they do life together, but they are committed to the cause of the gang much like the church should be to the mission of Christ.

What if our church community looked more like a gang. We would have meetings to see how everyone was doing and to remind each other of the mission we were on. We would organize strategies to fulfill the great commission and spur each other on to do good works. If anyone had an issue, everyone would come together to help meet that need. We would stay connected throughout the week and have get-togethers where our kids would play and our spouses would connect. We would love each other more than our own lives and push each other to go further in our walk with the Lord.

Is this not the picture of the church in Acts? Acts 4:32 says, *"Now the entire group of those who believed were of one heart and mind, and no one claimed that any of his possessions was his own, but instead they held everything in common."* If your church community looked like this, would it not be so attractive that everyone would want in? The people in your small groups would feel like they had a family in Christ. When one member is feeling too weak to go on, the others would help lift them up. They would strengthen each other in their time of need and encourage one another towards godliness.

Ecclesiastes 4:9-12 tells us, *"Two are better than one, because they have a better return for their labor."* We are not meant to go at this alone. Community was God's idea. Yes, we will all stand before the judgment seat of Christ by ourselves to give an account for every word and deed. But in this present day, we are meant to live the Christian life out *together*.

You might be thinking: "That all sounds great, but where do I start?" The only way your spiritual seed will grow, is when it has the right soil around it. Start by planting your seed surrounded by the soil of others who are passionately pursuing Christ, and watch as the growth takes place. You're possibly in a small group already, but it looks nothing like what I've described? Maybe you see each other once a week and do a topic study, then just go on your way? Or maybe you aren't plugged into a group at all. It all starts with removing the mask and letting people in. Find that one friend who is serious about their faith and ask them to start meeting and doing life together.

God's primary resource for meeting your needs are other believers! The problem is that many believers go to church and study groups wearing a superficial mask. Wanting to appear strong and together, they rob themselves of the opportunity of having their needs met in the warmth and safety of the Christian community. In the process, they rob their community of the opportunity to minister to their needs – one of the primary reasons God gathered us into churches in the first place. By denying other believers the privilege of meeting your legitimate needs, you are acting independently of God and you are vulnerable to getting your needs met by the world, the flesh and Satan.

Jesus prayed this prayer as he was approaching the cross:

"I pray not only for these, but also for those who believe in me through their word. May they all be one, as you, Father, are in me and I am in you. May they also be in us, so that the world may believe you sent me. I have given them the glory you have given me, so that they may be one as we are one. I am in them and you are in me, so that they may be made completely one, that the world may know you have sent me and have loved them as you have loved me."
John 17:20-23

Jesus prayed that the unity of His followers would be equal to the oneness of the Father and Son! He wants us to be one just as the Father and Son are united. We cannot accomplish this outside of true community. Jesus even goes on to say that it is through this unity that people outside the church would come to believe that He is the Messiah sent by God. To be all different stones that make up the Temple of God where Christ is the corner stone. This kind of oneness is what God desires for His church!

A New Family

Let me to tell you a story about Chris. Chris grew up without a father, and was abused verbally and physically by several of his mother's boyfriends as a child. He got into drugs at the young age of 9 and ended up being expelled from school by the age of 16. The only male figures in his life would constantly talk down to him. They would say that there was nothing good in him and never would be. As Chris grew up, he started believing what they said. Working long hours everyday of the week, Chris put his job before everyone and everything.

Chris met his first wife through a friend from work. She got pregnant 2 months into them meeting and then again a couple months after having their first child. He felt trapped, so they got married because it seemed like the right thing to do. Chris would spend all his time either at work or at the bars to escape his responsibilities as a husband and a father.

On June 13, 2013, Chris got a call from his neighbor telling him there had been an accident and he needed to come home. Chris didn't care and hung up the phone. The neighbor called him back and told him that he needed to come home right away, that his youngest son had died. After the incident, DCS stepped in and took his other son away and his wife's two daughters as well. Six months later they came back with an autopsy report showing that his baby died from an overdose of morphine and ruled his death a murder.

The next thing that Chris knew, he was locked up behind bars on a murder charge that he knew nothing about. A year in, Chris's mom was able to get him out on bail. It turned out that his wife was drugging their son to get him to stop crying and make him sleep. His sentence got reduced to child neglect and he got a second chance at life.

As soon as Chris got out of jail, he started the process of trying to get the son back that DCS took away. A few months after his release from jail, Chris met a girl named Cassidy. At some point, Cassidy's mom told her she needed to leave Chris or move out of her house. She decided to move out and move in with him. They were a couple years into dating and she gave birth to their daughter Sofia. Chris was getting 2 hours of supervised visits with his son every other weekend by now. He hadn't changed much as a person by this time. He was still living for himself, either drowning himself in work or out doing drugs while Cassidy raised their daughter. In the midst of all of this, Chris knew he needed a change. He decided that he needed a new job that didn't require so much overtime and weekends.

During his job search, Chris received multiple offers. For some reason, the one he felt drawn to was offering a lot less money than the others. He took the job and started working with a guy named Darren who I introduced you to earlier in the book. Our group was communicating daily through a video chat discussing several different topics and Scriptures. Chris was stuck in the van with Darren listening to all of these guys talk about faith, Scripture, and real life struggles. Darren invited Chris to come check out the men's group several times before he agreed.

His first night in group, Chris felt like God was telling him to open up and share his story. He began to share in tears and spilled his guts to this room full of men that he had never even met before. He talked about his son who died, his jail time, his current struggle with weed, and several other things. He felt loved and accepted for one of the first times in his life. He decided to continue coming back to group and started attending church with us on the weekends.

One day in group, he was talking about his struggles with smoking weed and his desire to quit. We encouraged him to delete all of the dealers numbers out of his phone. He couldn't do it. He walked up to me at the end of group and handed me his phone. On the screen were 17 numbers highlighted and ready to delete, but he couldn't push the button. I gladly deleted them from his contacts that night.

Soon enough, Chris made a decision to follow Christ. He began reading his Bible and praying daily. Cassidy was not too happy with his new found faith and didn't want him to continue. She had some bad experiences with church in her past and wanted nothing to do with it. One night, they had a huge fight and she went to pack her stuff and leave. As she was in the bedroom going through their stuff, Chris felt the nudge to go talk to her. He went in the room and sat on the bed. They had a long talk and the Holy Spirit began speaking directly through him to Cassidy. After some persuasion, she agreed to start reading the Bible and coming to church with him to see for herself if this was real. She couldn't deny the change that she was seeing take place in Chris right before her eyes.

Pretty soon, she was coming to my wife, Halee's women's group and opening up about her own issues. God softened her heart and drew her to Himself. She decided that she wanted to have this relationship with Jesus like she saw in Chris and these women in the group. Not long after this commitment, Chris asked Cassidy to marry him and she said, "Yes".

One weekend, a bunch of us from the different groups planned a kayak trip for my wife's birthday. We were jamming out to worship music while floating down the river, just having a blast. At one point when we pulled over to the side, Chris and Cassidy decided that they wanted to get baptized by Darren and Halee. What an honor! They got baptized, and declared their commitment to following Christ. It was an amazing day.

Meanwhile, Chris had been in the process of trying to get his son back for 5 years now. Several people including his lawyer were telling him that he may never get more than supervised visits and tried to talk him into giving up. He came to group one night and said he was considering throwing in the towel. Everyone in group told him that was the wrong decision. We told him that it was always too soon to quit. He ended up agreeing and said that he was going to keep pursing custody. We all prayed with him about the situation and the mediation meeting that was scheduled for later that week. Chris went into that meeting and everything was different. For the first time ever, they began to see things from his perspective and the legal guardian of his son was willing to meet him halfway. They agreed to give unsupervised visits for the first time starting the next weekend. These visits that would increase in length every couple weeks and eventually be overnight stays. This was a miracle! This was the favor of God!

The next thing that needed to happen was for them to have a wedding. They didn't have the money for some big wedding, but Chris wanted Cassidy to have the wedding of her dreams. Several of the men and women from the groups started brainstorming to figure out a way to make it all happen. Josh and Kenzie, who I introduced you to in chapter 2 of the book, moved all of their furniture out of their living room and made it into the perfect reception area. Several of us went and helped decorate and setup into the morning hours the night before the wedding. One of the guys in group is a licensed pastor who does weddings and he volunteered to marry them as well as provide the pre-marital counseling. They found a beautiful pavilion in a park that was surrounded by a pond and perfect for the wedding venue. This was nothing that had to be booked, so it was free as well. The wedding ceremony was absolutely incredible and intimate. We were all able to circle around them and lay hands on them as we prayed blessings over their marriage. The reception was one of the best parties I have ever been to. This community of believers is truly one of the best things that has ever happened to us and our family.

About a week prior to the wedding, Chris decided that he wanted to get his broken tooth fixed for the pictures. He didn't have much money to fix it, but we insisted that he go to the dentist to find out what it would cost. Prior to the visit, Josh called the dentist and told him Chris' story and said that he would like to pay for the tooth repair. The whole group pitched in money and paid for him to get his tooth fixed before the wedding. When Chris went in, the dentist fixed the tooth on the spot and said, you're all finished and ready to go. He asked how much he owed the dentist and he told him it was taken care of already.

Chris is now a big part of our church's jail ministry. He goes into the very same jail that he spent time in and leads Bible studies with the inmates. He has also started a group like ours on another night of the week for men fresh out of jail. Chris has a heart for these men and can connect with them in a way that many people cannot. He is growing so much through serving that it's truly inspiring. Being responsible for leading a study has pushed him to dig deeper into the Word and study the Scriptures harder than ever.

I share Chris' story with you because this is what community is supposed to look like. We are to come together as many members of one body. If one part of the body is hurting then the whole body suffers. We are to lift each other up and encourage one another. We are to teach, love, and disciple one another. At times, we are to correct and rebuke one another as well. You're not able to speak into someones life in that way unless you have established a true relationship first. That happens in community.

Jesus frees us from being orphans in this world to being children of God. He places us into a body of believers to aid us in our journey, and to go out and spread His love and extend His Kingdom. If we are going make a mark on this world for Jesus, then we need to band together. Two is better then one, remember? Get plugged into a body of believers this week. Live life as Jesus' hands, feet, and mouthpiece to go out and change the world around you. We are called to be salt and light. It starts with you!!!

Jesus Frees Us

"It is a joy to Jesus when a person takes time to walk more intimately with Him. The bearing of fruit is always shown in Scripture to be a visible result of an intimate relationship with Jesus Christ."
Oswald Chambers

9

Intimacy With Christ

"Call to me and I will answer you and tell you great and incomprehensible things you do not know."
Jeremiah 33:3

Do you cry out to God when you are alone? Do you seek Him in the secret place of prayer so that He can reveal the deep and hidden things of His heart to you? Jesus tells us, *"On that day many will say to me, 'Lord, Lord, didn't we prophesy in your name, drive out demons in your name, and do many miracles in your name?' Then I will announce to them, 'I never KNEW you. Depart from me, lawbreakers." Matthew 7:22,23 (my emphasis added).* So, it's not just those who profess to believe in and know of Jesus that inherit eternal life, but those who *know* Him and are *known* by Him. So my question would be, do you truly *know* Him and are you deeply *known* by Him?

In Matthew 1:23-25, it says that Joseph took Mary as his wife but did not *know* her until after she gave birth to her son. The use of this word *know* obviously means to *know* intimately. Mary was having a baby even though she had never *known* a man. So when Jesus says that many will call Him Lord on that day and He will reply that He never *knew* them, we can see that He desires more than just a superficial type of knowledge.

It's A Love Relationship

When I started dating my wife, I would ask her friends what she liked and stalk her social media to find out more about her, but I didn't truly know her. To get to know her, I had to spend time with her. I was infatuated by her and longed to get to know her more deeply. I pursued her intentionally because I wanted to win her heart and have her as my own. Does your relationship with Christ look anything like a love relationship? Do you have a craving for His presence in your life? To get to know Jesus, we have to spend quality time with Him.

If you're like the majority of Christians today, then you may not even know what having a relationship with Jesus looks like. Maybe you had a desire to know the Lord, but lately you've lost it and grown cold. Your Bible reading is mundane and dry if not non-existent. Your prayers are short and either at bedtime or over meals. You have lost your first love.

You want to have the benefits of God's provision and protection in your life, but have no desire for His presence in your life. Are you satisfied with something less than God wants for you?

Throughout the New Testament, Jesus refers to the church as His bride. He wanted a people of His own that He could share His heart with. A people with such a craving for His Word and such a passion for prayer that they couldn't even imagine going a day without it. Every moment spent with Him makes the cravings grow stronger and stronger. Where is the affection, the love, the craving in your heart? Where is the love a son should have for the Father who adopted him? It's comparable to the longing a bride should have to be with her groom.

If you have grown cold in your heart for the presence of God, then it's time to re-establish your commitment. It is time to get rid of every attachment to the things of this world and everything that stands between your abiding relationship with the Lord. The time for half-hearted devotion to Christ is over. He never called for anyone to marvel at Him from a distance. He wanted a people that would pursue Him and take up their cross to walk alongside Him. A people that would lovingly chase after Him with all their heart, mind, and strength. This is a love affair!

Direct Access

From the Old Testament scriptures all the way up to the crucifixion of Christ, there was an inner chamber in the temple of God. This chamber was known as the Holy of Holies. It was a room separated from the rest of the temple where the ark of the covenant was kept and could not be entered but once a year by the high priest. The high priest was the only one allowed to enter the Holy of Holies and only on the Day of Atonement to offer a sacrifice for his sins and the sins of the people. A large veil covered the entrance to this room so no one could see in. God said that He would appear in the Holy of Holies, hence the need for the veil. Before the high priest entered this chamber on the Day of Atonement, he had to wash himself, put on special clothing, bring burning incense for the smoke to cover his eyes from a direct view of God, and bring sacrificial blood with him to make atonement for sins. He would also wear bells on his robe with a rope tied around his waist to drag him out in case he fell over dead. No one could see God and live. His awesome presence was too much for a sinful man to look upon.

There was this barrier between all people and God until the death of Jesus. When Jesus was hanging on the cross and cried out in a loud voice, *"It Is Finished"* and breathed His last breath. The veil was torn in two from top to bottom. Because of the death of Jesus on the cross, man is no longer separated from God.

"We have boldness to enter the sanctuary through the blood of Jesus- he has inaugurated for us a new and living way through the curtain (that is, through his flesh)"
Hebrews 10:19-20.

The Holy of Holies, the very presence of God, is now open to all who are in Christ. Not only that, but God sent His Spirit to live inside of us. We are the new temple, the temple of the Holy Spirit. Do you catch the significance of that? This area that no one was able to enter because of the awesome presence of God is now *in us!*

Because of Christ's sacrifice on the cross, we now have direct access to the throne of God. Hebrews 4:16 says we can now come boldly to the throne of grace. We can enter into this throne room surrounded by angels and a great cloud of witnesses and the very presence of God to commune with Him. This is not the throne of performance or perfection, it is the throne of *grace*. Our approaching the throne is not dependent upon our character, but upon our position. If we are *in* Christ, then God doesn't see our sinfulness but only Christ's perfection. We can approach His throne knowing that by Jesus' sacrifice we are perfected *forever*. (See Hebrews 10:14) We take this for granted and settle for a short bedtime prayer and a couple of verses in our devotional. We rely on preachers and their sermons to tell us about God when we have a direct line to the Father. We are content with getting a message from God second hand when God says *"Come and sit with me, enjoy my presence."*

"Keeping our eyes on Jesus, the source and perfecter of our faith. For the joy that lay before him, he endured the cross, despising the shame, and sat down at the right hand of the throne of God." Hebrews 12:2.

What was this joy that Jesus foresaw? It was not only to sit down at the right hand of the throne of God. It was also a pure virgin bride, undefiled by the world and deeply in love with her bridegroom. It was a closeness unlike anything we have ever experienced before. It was an intimacy of being one with His creation. This is what we were made for. We were made for Him, to abide in Him, and by His holy presence to be conformed into His image.

If you have been married for any amount of time, then you and your spouse have probably conformed into each other's image a little bit. What I mean is that my wife and I now finish each other's sentences. Halee never liked seafood when we met, but I loved it. Now she loves it too and her favorite meal is the salmon that I cook. I didn't like anything spicy when we met, but she did. Now I can't get enough, and actually eat more spicy foods than her. There are things about each of us that have conformed into a likeness of one another simply from spending so much time together throughout the years. That is what happens as we spend more and more time in the presence of Jesus. We are conformed into His image and become more like Him. We desire what He desires and are grieved by what grieves Him.

Desiring Him Above All Else

The men of God in the Old Testament knew the value of God's presence. Moses knew that without the presence of God, neither he nor the nation could make it through the hard times to come. "Then Moses said to him, *'If your presence does not go with us, do not send us up from here.'" Exodus 33:15.* When Nehemiah chose to go and rebuild the wall around Jerusalem he told the people, *"Set your heart and soul to seeking the Lord your God." 1 Chronicles 22:19.* Though David was a great king and warrior, he said to the Lord, *"One thing I ask of the Lord, this is what I seek: that I may dwell in the house of the Lord all the days of my life, to gaze upon the beauty of the Lord and to seek him in his temple." Psalm 27:4.* Scripture says that Enoch *"walked with God, and he was no more because God took him." Genesis 5:21.* It's as if God was saying, *"There is no closer intimacy for me to have with you in time Enoch. So come and be with Me in eternity."* This kind of intimacy is a close personal communion between God and these men. They had it, and the veil wasn't even torn yet! They looked forward to our day in anticipation and rejoiced.(Jn. 8:56)

This relationship comes when we desire the Lord more than anything else in this life. To want to walk with the Lord in purity and righteousness. To be sanctified and refined. To be shaped and molded into what we were created to be. To have everything that is unlike Jesus chiseled away until all people can see is Him. You cannot get that intimacy from other people, sermons and preachers. You have to go straight to the source. You have to sit at the feet of Jesus and wait upon Him in that secret place where it's just you and Him.

"Jesus will not abide in a temple that ignores Him."
David Wilkerson.

Do you want to live a fruitful life for Jesus? Do you want a life marked by abundant provision and great and mighty works for God? Do you want to be a branch that overflows with so much fruit, that you can't store it all? David Wilkerson, the author of <u>The Cross And The Switchblade</u>, said after all his traveling and being known around the world as a man of God; after building buildings and becoming what many referred to as famous, he lost the touch of God. He said that he had the anointing and he knew when it was lifted. He had to get it back no matter the cost. Even with all the things he had accomplished for the kingdom of God, and the name he had made for himself, he knew that none of that mattered apart from *knowing* God intimately.

Now here's something that David Wilkerson said that has stuck with me and has pushed me to *know* God more intimately for myself. He said, *"All true ministry comes out of an intimacy with Christ."* I repeat... *"All true ministry comes out of an intimacy with Christ."* If you don't have godliness, you don't have a ministry. So if your ministry comes from any other place, all your works will be burned. If I want to have a life-changing ministry, then it can come from no other place than an intimate relationship with the life-changer Himself.

Beholding Christ

The word "Beholding" in Greek means to *fix our gaze*. Our character is formed and changed by whatever obsesses us. We are all being changed, but what are we being changed by? *What are you fixing your gaze on?* You have to have the character before you can have the impact. If your character has not been formed and God uses you in a mighty way, you may get prideful and take credit rather than give God the glory.

How does your character get formed? Your character is formed as you go through trials and look to Jesus and His Word. It is formed through the fiery furnace of affliction as you determine to not move from your position until God gives you something in His presence that changes you. As you go through the valley, you look to Him to supply all of your needs, to tell you where to go, what to do and to give you direction. You no longer lean on your own understanding because you have been in His presence. You have tasted and seen that the Lord is good. Your ministry now is to get alone with Him and behold His face. This is the ministry that all believers are called to.

Do you seek God with all that you have? Do you pray that He will give you revelation? God says, *"If you seek Him, He will be found by you, but if you abandon Him, He will abandon you."* 2 *Chronicles 15:2.* This is a solemn warning. We cannot go on as if it's business as usual. There must be a change in how we do things. There must be a new passion and urgency in how we approach the Lord. He wants to be so close to you, but you forsake Him for other things. Social media and television have taken all of our time and we haven't left any time for God. It's time for us to say enough is enough. We need to cut off everything standing between us and God and seek Him with all that we have.

Surrounded By Answered Prayers

Allow me to tell you about a dear friend of mine named Debbie. She's someone that I view as the very definition of a prayer warrior. She's one of those people that you can just see Jesus in her without her saying a word. A person who deeply *knows* and is deeply *known* by God. I met her many years ago in the morning prayer meetings that I began to attend at our church. Whenever I heard her pray, it was as if I could feel heaven opening up in the room. When I asked her about the intimacy she has with Jesus in her times of prayer, she said, *"For me, the most intimate part of prayer is hearing the voice of my Beloved."* In the most intimate writings of the Bible, the Song of Solomon pens the words *"kol dodi"*, translated *"The voice of my Beloved"*. Debbie told me as she began to reminisce upon her journey in learning to pray, and hear God's voice, she heard Him say to her, *"I've loved revealing My heart to you for the past 24 years."* Is that not the essence of intimacy? The revealing of the heart from one to another… Does it not bring you to a place of awe in knowing that the Creator of your soul desires this type of relationship with you?

Debbie was raised in a home where the knowledge of God was present, but her parents were emotionally absent. In an upbringing where the religious training lacked parental intimacy, it was little more than following rules to her. When Debbie grew up, she entered into a marriage with a huge emotional and religious black hole within herself. That void would continually cry out to be filled. As it remained unfilled, she found herself desperately jumping into darkness with a pursuit of intimacy in all the wrong places. As Debbie says, *"Even private sins have a way of being made very public and even more painful."* Her marriage ended and as her sins came out, the few close friends she had at the time began to leave as well.

As always, God had a greater purpose for her life. His message through Hosea to a wayward Israel was the same message He began to speak to Debbie.

"He led me into the wilderness and spoke tenderly to me... and made the valley of trouble a door of hope."
Hosea 2:14-15.

God brought her to a desert place where all her dependence was on Him to create the most intimate bond with Himself. Without a spouse or any close friends, she found herself crying out to God over every detail of her life. In this desert place of being shut in with God, she found these words from Isaiah to reign true. *"For the High and Exalted One, who lives forever, whose name is holy, says this: 'I live in a high and holy place, and with the oppressed and lowly of spirit, to revive the spirit of the lowly and to revive the heart of the oppressed."* Isaiah 57:15. She not only had to deal with her own emotional burdens, but also those of her 12, 14, and 16 year old kids at the time. They were having to cope with the failures of both parents as well as their whole routine and way of living being completely flipped upside down.

Debbie's children were home schooled their whole lives up to this point. The year prior to all of this happening, they purchased a kit to stencil the constellations on their bonus room ceiling. The florescent paint marked out several groupings of stars such as Orion, Ursa Major, Cephas and other beautiful symbols of God's perfect created order and purpose in the universe. A year later, on her darkest spiritual night, the Lord reminded Debbie of this same truth in her own life. Even in the midst of all her brokenness, God was still faithfully orchestrating every event of her life for His purposes.

During one of her kids weekends away, Debbie walked into their seemingly vacant bonus room; but it wasn't completely empty. She looked up to the ceiling at what represented the perfect order of the heavens shining down upon her and she suddenly had an inspiration. She went to her bedroom and thought about one of God's most recent answers to her prayers. She took the florescent paint and put a single dot there in the middle of her bedroom ceiling. This would become her altar of remembrance for God's faithfulness in her life. A way of reminding her fearful heart that He was present even in the darkness. As she continued to present requests to her Heavenly Father, day after day He answered. Night after night, the ceiling of her bedroom would gain new lights. On nights when everyone was asleep or away, and loneliness would start to creep in, she could stare up to the ceiling and be reminded of God's ever-present care for her and her children.

At times, her teenagers would come in and turn off the lights to marvel at this visible reminder. Their earthly father may have left, but their Heavenly Father was still watching over them. Many times, they would come in to stand on the bed and paint their own touches of gratitude on the ceiling. When a significant provision for their family would occur, they would create a spiral galaxy or a shooting star. It became their family's own Sistine Chapel of thanksgiving and praise. During nights that she would weep over her losses through tears, Debbie would be confronted with this growing universe glowing all around her.

Through the months, her intimacy grew deeper and deeper. Her character was being replaced more and more by His character. His answers to prayer were often accompanied with hearing His voice. At first, she heard His voice through His Word that she would read every morning and every night. Over time, she began to hear His personal voice reciting Scriptures in her head for the needs of herself and others. However, she says the most precious moments were those when she could hear His voice singing over her. Her prayers had moved from times of routine requests, to a continual communication with the Mighty Intimate One. He revealed Himself to her as her Protector, the One powerful enough to save her from her own destruction; and as her Beloved, the

One tender enough to hold her in His strong arms and sing softly in her ear.

He Is Enough

Jesus frees us from the separation that has plagued us since The Fall. This is the most precious gift of all, the gift of Himself. We no longer need a "Moses" to go up on the mountain and relay messages to us from God, because we have direct access to Him ourself. We are free to sit with Him and walk with Him. We are free to have a love relationship with the Creator of our souls. What could be better than that? If you are like so may others and have taken this for granted, repent and ask God to fill you with a craving for His presence today!

"Now without faith it is impossible to please God, since the one who draws near to him must believe that he exists and that he rewards those who seek him."
Hebrews 11:6

Jesus Frees Us

"The truth is that, though we were justified by faith alone, the faith that justifies is never alone [it always produces fruit, "good works"...a transformed life]."
J.I. Packer

10

Saving Faith

*"You believe that God is one. Good! Even the demons
believe-and they shudder."*
James 2:19

If the demons and Satan believe in God, yet
will never be saved, then what kind of belief or faith
will save you? Are we saved by grace alone, through
faith alone, in Christ alone, that no man may boast?
Or is faith without works dead and a man considered
righteous by what he does and not faith alone? Yes...
Both of these statements are accurate and both are
straight from Scripture. How can both of these
statements be true? Don't they obviously contradict

each other? No... With a little study and knowing the context and audience of both statements, they actually compliment and support one another.

From Righteousness, Not For Righteousness

In Ephesians 2:8,9 Paul says, *"For you are saved by grace through faith, and this is not from yourselves; it is God's gift—not from works, so that no one can boast."* Paul was refuting Jewish legalism in this statement. He was also showing that there is no amount of good that anyone could do to earn salvation. We cannot do enough good to outweigh the bad in our life, and we cannot earn God's favor. By definition, grace is a blessing that is undeserved and unwarranted. It is a gift freely given based on the kind intentions of the giver to a recipient who has no claim to it. We are saved not because we are good and deserving, but because God is *good* and *gracious*.

Paul's statement here in Ephesians doesn't end there though... Ephesians 2:10 says, *"For we are his workmanship, created in Christ Jesus for good works, which God prepared ahead of time for us to do."* You see, we are not saved by good works, but we are saved for good works. Scripture tells us to, *"make every effort (2 Peter 1;5), work out our salvation with fear and trembling (Philippians 2:12), strain towards what it ahead (Philippians 3:13), etc."* This is not to attain salvation, but this is after the point of salvation. This is our sanctifying work.

Let me explain what James means when he

says, *"You see that a person is justified by works and not by faith alone." James 2:24.* James was opposing something called *antinomianism.* This idea was the twisting of the faith that they had in Christ saying that no work was necessary. Paul meant that the works of the Mosaic law were no longer needed. James meant that our works are produced by our faith, and that they validate our faith in Christ as genuine. So to put it simply, it is not by works but [by grace through *faith* that we are saved]. If we are truly saved, then we will not use God's grace as an excuse to go on sinning. The truly born again believer will have *fruit* that they can be recognized by.

True belief is always followed by sincere action. If I truly believe that a car is going to hit me, then I will move out of the way. If I truly believe that my house is about to blow up, then I will get my family out of there as fast as possible. If I really think that the Word of God is absolute truth, then action will naturally follow that belief. Our works, deeds, and actions are the outward evidence (or the fruit) of what we really believe to be true.

A tree doesn't strain to produce a different kind of fruit than what it naturally produces. If we have an intimate relationship with Jesus, then good works will naturally flow out of that intimacy. If you have deeds but don't spend time with God and feel a true connection with Jesus, then stop doing works and get on your face before God. Be shut in with Him until He overflows out of you. If you do a lot of good works, but have no joy in serving, then you're doing it out of duty and not a truly regenerated heart. On one hand, sometimes we have to do things that we don't *feel* like doing simply out of obedience, and there is joy to be had in that. But what is the purpose of our good deeds if we are constantly growing distant from Him in the process? Our unity with Christ is far more important than simply getting lost in religious tasks.

God tells us, *"Be holy, because I am holy."* *1 Peter 1:16*. He isn't talking about legalism or moral perfection. There are two forms of holiness that a Christian must possess. *Positional* holiness and *personal* holiness. *Positional* holiness has to do with our salvation. *Personal* holiness has to do with our sanctification. *Positional* holiness says that we are made perfectly righteous through faith in Christ and His substitutionary work on the cross. *"He made the one who did not know sin to be sin for us, so that in Him we might become the righteousness of God."* *2 Corinthians 5:21. Personal* holiness means that we are now becoming in practice what God has already declared us to be in position. It is because we are *positionally* holy that we can pursue a life of *personal* holiness. We're not trying to be holy in order to attain or be made righteous. We work from righteousness, not for righteousness.

The Fruit, Not The Root

"Remain in Me, and I in you. Just as a branch is unable to produce fruit by itself unless it remains on the vine, neither can you unless you remain in Me." John 15:4

Can a branch bear fruit on it's own, or does the vine produce the fruit in the branch? You will not bear fruit unless you abide in the vine. Jesus is the vine. The branch's only duty is to stay connected to the vine. It is not to push out fruit by laboring. It is not to sprout green leaves. It is not to absorb nutrients from the ground. The vine provides all the nutrients needed to make the branch thrive and produce it's fruit. The branch is completely dependent on the vine, and we must be completely dependent on Jesus.

Speaking of fruit, *"The fruit of the Spirit is love, joy, peace, long suffering, kindness, goodness, faithfulness, gentleness and self-control." Galatians 5:22,23.* These are contrary to the acts of the flesh. In order to have true love, joy, peace, long suffering, kindness, goodness, faithfulness, gentleness and self-control, you must be walking according to the Spirit and truly abiding in Christ. The acts of the flesh and the fruit of the Spirit do not flow from the same stream. If you find the majority of your life being ruled by the flesh and overcome by sin, then you cannot be bearing true fruit for God. You may see areas of your life that look fruitful, but how can you bear fruit apart from the vine? You can't! You are doing it in your own strength, and if you can do that in your own strength, just imagine what you could accomplish when the Spirit of God is flowing through you. If you have what looks like fruit in your life apart from abiding in Christ, then it's dead and rotting fruit. It might look good and taste sweet at first bite, but it's going to leave a sour place in the end if it's not flowing from Jesus.

So should you do good works? Absolutely. Just remember that the deeds you do should be the outpouring of Jesus in your life. They are not meant to draw attention to you, but to Him. I'm seeing now more than ever, that this life of bearing fruit for God is a process. It is a marathon, not a sprint. The longer that we stay in close proximity with Christ, the more fruitful we will be. This is where a disciple of Christ is formed. Go there, live there, abide there, and you will bear fruit that will endure for eternity.

Obedience, Conviction, Dependence

The life of a true believer is marked by three things. Obedience, conviction, and dependence. If we have saving faith, then we will be taking steps of *obedience* towards God. Our lives will be lived intentionally for the King of kings. We will live in obedience to what His Word tells us to do. As a true born again believer, we will have *conviction* that does not allow us to continue on in willful sin. This conviction bears witness to our spirit that a superior Spirit is at work within us, the Holy Spirit of God. We won't be able to stay in sins of ignorance because God's Spirit will point them out to us.

We will also be *dependent* on Him and rest secure in His direction. This doesn't mean we don't have plans and goals of our own. Instead, it means that we are always willing and ready to surrender all the outcomes up to Him. Does this sound like you, or are you just going through the motions? The motions end in eternal separation. Faith that saves is knowing and being known by Jesus. It's a relationship.

If we know Him and love Him, we will be obedient to Him. This obedience will not come out of a sense of duty alone, but will be spurred on by the joy we have in Him. This joy comes from a knowledge of His truth, a faith in that truth and a relationship with the Author of Truth. It comes from what He has done and who He is, not what we have done and who we are. If we get our joy from our performance instead of from His performance then our joy will never be complete because our obedience will never be perfect. Joy in the firm foundation of who God is and what God has done will drive our obedience to what He says in His Word. If we are known by Him, then His Spirit dwells in us and convicts and directs us. Obedience follows faith and faith results in more obedience. Not out of duty but born out of relationship.

"Satan tells me I am unworthy; but I always was unworthy, and yet You have long loved me; and therefore my unworthiness cannot be a barrier to having fellowship with You now."
Charles Spurgeon

A good friend of mine sent me this quote the morning after a long day of struggling. It was a great reminder at the time because I was in the depths of despair, thinking I was failing God and needing to earn back His love. But Spurgeon is correct. I am unworthy and have always been unworthy. The devil cannot shame me with this news because it's actually the good news of the gospel.

Scripture says we overcome by the blood of the Lamb and the Word of our testimony. But what is our testimony? My testimony is that I was broken and God made me whole. I was lost and now I'm found. I was wretched, poor, and cut off, but now I am righteous, justified, and redeemed. I was blind, but now I see. My testimony is that I am unworthy and have always been unworthy, but Christ is worthy and it's in His worthiness that I stand. You see, the news of my unworthiness is the best news ever.

At the time of receiving that text, I was trying to live this holy and righteous life, but pride and false humility was flaring up inside of me. I thought, *"Man, I'm doing pretty good!"* Just when I thought I was standing on firm footing, it was actually the soil of a somewhat hardened heart. In that moment, God had to break up the ground to show me that it's only *in Him* that I can truly stand. Just like I could not attain this righteousness on my own, I cannot hold onto it by my own strength or by my own striving. It is not dependent on my getting better day after day or in my maturing and growing up. It is dependent on *whose* I am.

If my child is born with a cognitive disability, they do not stop being my child simply because they don't mature. We are no more His children as we mature than when we were first purchased. If we never "grow up," we are no less his kids. And if we never "do better," we are no less loved. However,

Jesus loves us so much that He will not leave us how He found us. He gives us His Holy Spirit who teaches us, convicts us, and guides us. The more we pay attention to Him, the more we grow. And the more we apply His Word to our lives, the more we mature.

God resists the proud and draws near to the humble. God also disciplines those He loves. He will humble us if we begin to get prideful, but it's for the purpose of growing and molding us. If we are in Christ, then we are already perfect in His sight in our spirit. The more we understand that we are unworthy and that only Christ is worthy, and the more we focus on Him, the better off we are because we stay humble.

As we keep our eyes on this truth we begin to live out our identity in Christ. Not through our own strength, but through the acknowledgment that we need His. We begin to live holy and righteous lives not because we have to, but because that is who we are, and we start to become in practice what we have already been made in position. A pear tree should not produce anything but pears. If a pear tree produces oranges, it is unnatural. The natural thing for a Christian to do is produce Christ-like behavior. That only happens through our unity with Christ, conformity to His Word, and through a humble pursuit.

The more I mature the more dependent I am on Him because He continues to shows me that I cannot do it on my own. The longer I try, the clearer this truth becomes. I am saved by grace through faith. Not through works so that I cannot boast. Jesus is worthy, and it is only in Him that I am whole.

A Growing Repentance

I remember when I first read the book of James. It felt like a swift kick in the butt at just the right time. It was a call to action that I very much needed. However, like many other people I know, I began to have doubts about whether I was even saved or not. A lot of people don't feel assured of their salvation, so they do good works to prove that they are saved and then they still aren't sure... So how do you know that you possess salvation? How do you examine yourself to see if you're in the faith? How do you have this blessed assurance? Is it based on the magnitude of your repentance? Is it based on the measure of your character? Does it rely on the greatness of your faith? Do I look at how hard I fight my flesh and how much I serve and if I have a deeper repentance than other people I know? Can I be sure because I have this faith that I know God can and will move mountains?

These things are all part of the sanctification process, but they don't determine our salvation. We don't look for assurance of salvation in our character, or the magnitude of our repentance, or the quality of our faith. We have our assurance when we look to the character and greatness of the One who our faith is in. It's not our ability to hang on to Him, it's His ability to hang on to us!

Repentance at the point of conversion can

simply be a change of the mind. *"I'm falling and I need a Savior!"* There are many Scriptures throughout the Bible that talk about and unpack the depths of repentance. However, to believe that a person is not "In Christ" until they are complete in this whole biblical process of repenting is ridiculous. Just as our faith in Him will continue to grow the more we experience Him and the more we come to know Him, our repentance will continue to grow as well. We don't expect the same thing out of our 3 year old that we do from our 10 year old. So why do we expect the same level of repentance from a new convert or infant in Christ as we do someone who has walked with the Lord for decades?

You won't know that you're "In Christ" because of the depth of your repentance and sanctification, but because it continues on. The evidence that you have passed through the small gate is that you're now walking in the narrow way. As you grow and dig into His Word, as you walk in the Spirit and trust in Him more, as you do these things your repentance and faith will mature and deepen, and that is how you can be sure that you are *in* Him and He is *in* you. It's not that we have achieved a certain level of holiness, it is that we have a *bent* towards holiness. Like I said, sanctification is a life-long process. It's not that we have attained it, but that we press on!

Sustainable Pursuit

I was speaking with a guy in my group named Tyson the other day about his walk with Christ over the past 9 years. His testimony is one of dramatic life change centered on Jesus, followed by a period of falling away and spiritual schizophrenia. During that time he would go from one extreme to the other with leading Sunday school one weekend to black out drunk and fighting in bars the next. This took a major toll on his marriage, but eventually he would come back to God to live a life of true surrender and submission. Tyson is now progressively growing in his relationship with Jesus and leading his family as well as other men towards Christ.

Why does that happen to so many? Why do we have this passionate pursuit that often burns out and then we recommit to Christ and maintain a steady growth? How do we go from on fire to burnt out so quickly? The way that Tyson explained this to me in his own experience was very enlightening, so I wanted to share it with you.

At the age of 23, Tyson was a married man and his wife had just given birth to their second son. He had recently joined the Marines and was living like a frat boy: drinking, partying and lying to his wife. That lasted for a while until he became tired of all the emptiness and consumed with anxiety about getting caught in a lie. His wife took him to church one Sunday and he felt conviction about the way he was living and the lack of spiritual leadership he had been providing for his family. He went to a Christian bookstore the next day and was directed to a book called <u>Crazy Love</u> by Francis Chan. Up until that point, Tyson had always viewed Christianity as a long list of do's and dont's that would determine where he end up for eternity. He was blown away at the emphasis that the book placed on God's love for him. As a result, he ended up giving his life to Christ.

Tyson became obsessed with his new found love relationship with Jesus, devoting more of his time, attention and energy to reaching the lost. It became his mission to share Jesus with his fellow Marines and everyone who God placed in his path. He felt this love from God and experienced Him working in mighty ways as he shared the gospel with fellow troops and friends throughout his community. People were coming to know the Lord through Tyson's witness and then, he was deployed. While overseas, he quickly became exhausted by the daunting task of spreading the gospel as there were no fellow Christians to support him and encourage him in pressing on.

When Tyson came back home, he quickly started hanging out with old friends again, and began to slowly slip back into the party scene. He still kept his religious priorities at the top of the list by going to church and telling people about Jesus. However, at the same time he made going to parties and hanging out with old friends a top priority as well. He was distracted and realized that he was trying to live with one foot in the Kingdom and one foot in the world. This realization drove him to commit all of his time and energy to serving at the church. He distanced himself from people who drew him away and was soon at church every night of the week. He filled his time with hosting Bible studies as well as serving in 3-4 different ministries. Everything was led by a do more, try harder mentality. There was no Spirit-filled or Spirit-led love for His Savior in all of his striving. He didn't even have time to pray or read his Bible because of all the ways he was trying to serve God in his own strength.

This led to a superficial connection with God. Whenever Tyson would mess up and sin, he didn't have a true relationship to fall back on. His relationship with Jesus was one built on performance and a sense of always failing to measure up. It was a relationship that knew little about grace and mostly about judgment. Whenever trials came up like the loss of his child or whenever he slipped up and sinned, he would get angry and push away from God. Instead of running back to Him, he would feel as though his sin made it impossible to talk with God. So time after time, he would run further away and make it worse.

Eventually, Tyson's life was in shambles and filled with depression and anxiety. He would go through cycles of hopelessness and shortly began to look back on what it was like when he first gave his life to Christ. He remembered wanting Jesus above everything else and learned how to become satisfied in God alone again. He realized that in those times he was at peace and comforted, and felt joy and love despite his circumstances. He began to wonder how he could get back to that place.

Soon, Tyson was on his knees crying out to God and digging into the Bible for answers. He started by placing God back on the throne of his heart. Instead of doing more and trying harder, he began to ask God what He would have him do and started listening to His direction. God brought him back to a church where he became a part of a men's group. This led him to the task of leading his family with courage. It was the first time that he began to actually lead his wife and kids with humility. Before, he was just doing everything he could to serve in the church and this left his family to fend for themselves. Now he was taking his God-given role as the spiritual leader in his home seriously. (Now we as men really get this term of spiritual leader screwed up. Jesus modeled what leadership looked like with humility and service. A better term for spiritual leader may be *servant* leader. After all, Jesus is our ultimate example.)

Tyson's walk is not perfect, but he's in love with Jesus and is passionately pursuing a sustainable relationship with his Savior. He now knows that he was bought at a price and his life is no longer his own.

So the overarching story of Tyson's walk with Jesus is this:

It started out like a relationship with a girlfriend that he would have second thoughts about before coming back and marrying her. At first, it was the newness of it all that was so exciting. He was obsessed over this girl and had this fire burning inside of him. He had to get to know everything he could about her to win her heart and have her as his own. He had to go above and beyond to convince this new love that he was worthy of her affection.

Somewhere along the way, Tyson started having commitment issues. He started to feel like it was too much work trying to hold onto this relationship and wondered if it was even worth it. As soon as small obstacles arose, he fell back into some of his old ways and the fire began to die out. Over time, her absence made his heart grow fonder and he began to miss the relationship he once had:

Now, he is in a long-term lasting covenant relationship with Jesus that is progressing day after day and is sustainable for the long haul. He's no longer worried about losing the relationship, but rather sees it as necessary to ask the hard questions and face trials as teachable moments. Those trials are approached with joy in knowing that he is learning how to love Jesus better as he would learn to love a spouse and make his foundation of faith stronger. Along with viewing his commitment to Jesus in the same way as a marriage, Tyson is learning to submit more fully to Him as Lord of his life while being led by the Spirit in his daily walk.

You Can Know

Jesus frees us from an uncertainty of our eternal destination. We can know where our spirit will reside before we get there. Jesus said, *"The Kingdom of God is in your midst." Luke 17:21.* This means that we don't have to die to possess this Kingdom. Jesus pours out His Spirit on us and we can have eternal security and assurance now. If you haven't received the free gift of salvation, don't wait any longer. Today is the day of salvation! Don't put your head on your pillow tonight without knowing where you'll end up. Ask Jesus to come into your life and spend the rest of your days following hard after Him!

Jesus Frees Us

"Beginning well is a momentary thing. Finishing well is a lifelong thing."

Ravi Zacharias

11

Finishing Well

"Not that I have already reached the goal or am already perfect, but I make every effort to take hold of it because I also have been taken hold of by Christ Jesus. Brothers and sisters, I do not consider myself to have taken hold of it. But one thing I do: Forgetting what is behind and reaching forward to what is ahead, I pursue as my goal the prize promised by God's heavenly call in Christ Jesus.'
Philippians 3: 12-14

What does it mean to finish well? What does it mean to leave a legacy? How can we be ready to cross that finish line and hear the Judge say, *"Well done good and faithful servant."*? We all started this race at the point of surrendering our life to Christ, but how do we finish it in a manner worthy of the crown? I hope to answer all of these questions for you within this chapter.

Can God Really Use Me?

As I look back over my life at all of the different goals I've had and all of the temporary things I've chased after, I begin to hang my head. I often times look at all of my failures and begin to think that somehow I have been disqualified for the prize. I think that I've been disqualified to be used by God for anything of significance. I also think sometimes, that I've been disqualified to leave any kind of legacy that I could pass down to my children.

Then I remember all the people that God used throughout history and how damaged and unqualified many of them were.

People like Moses who was a murderer and weak in speech, yet God used him to rescue His people from the hands of the most powerful person in the world at that time, Pharaoh.

People like Samson, with a lust and discernment issue, yet God used him to wipe out a godless nation.

People like Paul, who claimed to be the chief of sinners and who persecuted Christ's church (aka. The Bride), yet God used him to plant churches, minister to the Gentiles and write two thirds of our New Testament.

It reminds me that God is in the business of using *nobodies*. I actually believe that God chooses to only use the broken people who acknowledge that they walk with a limp because He gets all the glory. The thorns in our flesh keep us utterly dependent on Him, and that's a good place to be.

I think it's safe to say that none of us are disqualified to be used of God. It doesn't matter how deep in the pit we are, Jesus is deeper still. There are no depths that we can plunge where Jesus cannot meet us there and pull us out! He can change us, mold us, and make us into more than we ever imagined!

Before I get into what it means to finish well, lets talk about some things that finishing well is not. Finishing well is not having the biggest house or the nicest car. It's not having the most money in your bank account or the most followers on Instagram. It's not possessing the most toys or being able to pay for your kid's college. These things aren't necessarily bad in and of themselves, but they won't last. You can't take them with you when you die, yet these are the types of things that society tells us matters the most. A lot of Christians may go as far as to tell you this world has nothing to offer. I submit to you that this world has a lot to offer. I'd even say that there's a lot that this world can give you to make you happy. However, the thing is, all of what this world has to offer is *temporary*

Temporary happiness and *temporary* fulfillment that in the end leaves you empty and found *wanting*. It's just stuff and it will all be in a landfill or a fire one day. So I challenge you to fix your eyes on what's *eternal* and what will last forever.

Finish The Race

"I have glorified you on the earth by completing the work you gave me to do." John 17:4

Jesus only lived 33 years, yet he finished the course marked out for him. Its not the quantity of life, but the quality of life that counts. Finishing well means living well today. Some people put off following Jesus when they're young and say they'll get to that when they're older. Our life is a vapor that is here today and gone tomorrow. We aren't promised to grow older and it's time to get right with God today. We get one chance at this life and we need to make it count. This life is a preparation for the next. We must finish well here on earth to begin well in eternity. The finish line is just the beginning.

At the 1968 Olympics in Mexico during the marathon event, a runner from Tanzania finished dead last, well behind all of the other runners. An Ethiopian runner crosses the finish line to win the race and the crowd erupts.

Way back on the track is John Stephen Akwhari of Tanzania. He has been lapped by several runners at this point. After 30 kilometers his head is throbbing, his muscles are aching and he falls to the ground in pain. He has serious leg injuries and the officials want him to retire, but he refuses. With his knee bandaged up, Akwhari picks himself back up and continues on. He hobbles the remaining 12 kilometers to the finish line an hour after the winner has crossed. Most of the crowd had already gone home at this point. Akwhari moved around the track at a snails pace, until finally collapsing over the finish line.

Afterwards, asked by a reporter why he had not dropped out, Akwhari says, *"My country did not send me to start the race. They sent me to finish."*

It doesn't matter how strong you start, it's how you finish. You could have done everything absolutely horrible up to this point, but you can start over! As long as you're still breathing, it's never too late to start again. Jesus said, *"The first will be last and the last will be first."* It doesn't matter when you finish, but that you finish well. When you cross that finish line and enter into glory, it won't matter the mistakes that you made throughout your life as long as you left them under the blood of Jesus. His blood covers you and cleanses you. His Spirit empowers you to walk in a new way. A narrow way that forgets what is behind, and strains towards the prize that you were created for. That prize is Jesus!

Leaving a Legacy

I want to leave a legacy that my children and

grandchildren can follow after. A legacy that isn't centered on me, but on Jesus. To lead a life that gives them confidence in the Lord's work and trust in His sovereign plan for their own life. To lead a life that inspires them to live radically for the Kingdom and to go further then I can ever go. Like Paul, I want to be able to look at my children and say, *"Imitate me as I also imitate Christ." 1 Corinthians 11:1.*

Definition of **Legacy**- *a gift or property that is handed down, endowed or conveyed from one person to another. It is something descendible that one comes into possession of that is inherited or received from a predecessor.*

By this definition of legacy, something is handed down of monetary value: property, money, an estate, a trust, etc. The type of legacy we are discussing is one of eternal value. To leave this kind of legacy, we must do at least five things through the course of our lives. We must die to ourselves, radically obey Jesus wherever He leads, invest in people, live lives that are above reproach, and finish well. Let's break these down one-by-one.

Dying To Self

To *die to self* means to lay down all of ones goals and aspirations. To hand over one's own desires and will in order to be subject to the Master's will. As Jesus said in the Garden of Gethsemane, *"Not my will, but yours, be done." Luke 22:42.* Jesus tells us in the gospels, *"If anyone wants to follow after me, let him deny himself, take up his cross daily, and follow me." Luke 9:23.*

To leave behind a legacy that is centered on Jesus, we must die to our own selfish desires in order to center everything we do around His desires. If we want to give our kids a confidence in His work and His plan, then we need to bring them in on what He is inviting us into. And what is He inviting us into? I would submit to you that it is the "*Kingdom*"—not heaven in the sky, but His activity here and now! This involves including them in on the questions and concerns that you bring to God. Modeling moment-to-moment dependence on God, and discussing with your family the experiences you have with God.

When I first started following Jesus, I felt as if I was a rocket ship going a thousand miles per hour and leaving everyone behind. I didn't understand that part of leading my family meant including them in on the process. I had a bad habit of assuming that everyone saw things from my perspective, and that they understood things the same way I did. If something in a song or a sermon jumped out to me, I just assumed that it hit them in the same way. I am learning that when I have those revelations from God, I need to share them with others. I need to explain exactly what He is speaking to me in order for them to understand and grow with me.

Radical Obedience

The things that we consider radical today appear to have been standard for the first century Christians. Things such as not considering anything we have as our own, but as a means to help and bless others. Things like living out all of the truths we find in Scripture. Like obeying what God puts on your heart immediately and without question. Things like sharing our faith with strangers and living as if the promises in His Word are trustworthy and true.

I remember when Darren first got saved. We would call him "Yes Man", because it was like he couldn't say no to anything we suggested him to do. If we told him to confess a struggle to his wife, he would go home and do it. If we told him that he should take a discipleship or apologetics class, then he would go and sign up. If we told him to pray with his coworkers, he did it the next day and everyday after. He said that God didn't want him to say no to anything that would grow him as a Christian, and so he didn't. That is radical obedience. That is radically following Christ without boundaries.

Let me share a quote with you that wrecked me when I heard it:

"Imagine this for a moment... God stands there on the day of Creation, and He tells planets to put themselves in certain orbits in space, and they all bow down and say Amen and Obey Him. He tells stars to find their place in the sky and to follow His decree to the letter, and they all bow down and Obey Him. He tells mountains to be lifted up and valleys to be cast down, and they bow down and worship. He tells the brave sea, "You will come to this point and you will come no further!", and the sea adores. And yet God tells you to come and you have the audacity to say NO!" -Paul Washer

So you see, when we talk about radically following Christ, it's actually what God expects. This shouldn't be the anomaly, but the norm. To be a disciple of Jesus means to abandon your old way of life and to actually *Follow Him*. If we are going to leave a legacy of *following* Jesus, then we have to get this right. How will your children take this thing seriously if you do not?

Investing In Others

When Jesus rose from the grave and stood on the mountain getting ready to ascend into heaven, He gave His followers one final decree. We call it the Great Commission. Jesus said, *"All authority has been given to me in heaven and on earth. Go, therefore, and and make disciples of all nations, baptizing them in the name of the Father and of the Son and of the Holy Spirit, teaching them to observe everything I have commanded you. And remember, I am with you always, to the end of the age."* *Matthew 28:18-20.* The most important thing we can do as Christians is to make disciples. Making disciples of Jesus is what will change the world. We spend so much time defending what we have the right to do, while neglecting what Jesus has commanded us to do. If we want to leave a legacy that will last into eternity, then we've got to start investing in other people.

Jesus had a small group. He would preach to the thousands, but He did life with a small group of men. He spent 3 years investing heavily into the lives of a core group of followers who would go on to change the world. Those three years of His life and teachings are still being studied and broken down 2000 years later. If we want our life to outlast us, then we need to spend it pouring into others. You would be surprised how much a cup of coffee and a 30 minute conversation would encourage someone in their walk.

Love people. I recently read about a pastor who would write *Love the People* at the top of his sermon notes so that he didn't forget the heart of his message. If we don't genuinely care about people, then they won't genuinely care about what we have to say either.

Above Reproach

To live above reproach doesn't mean to always get it right. It doesn't mean that we don't slip and fall at times. It's not about being perfect so that we can preach perfection. It's about being honest about where we fall short so there is no secret thing waiting to be found out. Let people in close enough to see the real you, and constantly be evaluating yourself through the lens of Scripture.

Wearing a mask and living the lie becomes more debilitating as time goes on. We apply layers upon layers to cover up our true selves with all of our struggles, fears and doubts that we don't want others to see. Underneath all of the layers is the person we truly are. We are fearfully and wonderfully made. God doesn't say that we *were* fearfully and wonderfully made *before we screwed it all up*. He says that we *are* fearfully and wonderfully made.

Looking back over my life, I can see seasons where I applied layers upon layers of cover-up to avoid discovery. Thankfully, I can also remember the moments where God chipped away at me to reveal what was hidden underneath. As a leader, I am constantly telling my story to different groups of men. Over and over again, I am sharing with them about the layers of lies I've covered myself with and the ways God has cracked through each and every one of them. I invite others to pick up a chisel, and in a safe place with the help of Jesus, begin to chip away at the lies they've applied over the years to their own hearts so that their true identity can be revealed. Once the layers are removed and we stand exposed in full view of our Creator, we can begin to live out the life we were created for. Only then can we live above reproach. If we are going to leave a legacy worth following, we must get rid of every hidden thing.

We've all done things in our life that we aren't proud of, that we regret. There are things I've done that I wish I could go back and undo, but even God can't change the past. We have to forget what is behind and strain towards what is ahead. Whatever we become in life is not nearly as important as the life we live and how we get there. Finishing well is living well today. This takes intentionality. This takes keeping God as *The Priority* in your life that all other priorities flow from. It takes finding your identity in Him and not the things of this world. It's not about being perfect. We can't earn God's favor, nor does He want us to. He has already paid the price through the blood of His Son. There is power in the blood. Through His blood, we are given eternal life and freedom from the bondage of sin. Jesus frees us and sets us on the track to run a new race. It is not for the purpose of starting the race, but for the purpose of finishing the race.

Finishing Well

We focus a lot on getting to the cross for our salvation, but we often neglect what comes after that. Having our sins forgiven is only half the gospel. The Kingdom of God is not simply where we go when we die. The Kingdom of God is living a resurrected life now! It's not enough to just come to the cross. We must die on that cross and go through that cross with Jesus into newness of life under the power of His Spirit. To finish this life well, we must lay aside the sins that so easily entangle us, take hold of Jesus and His Word, and press on to the finish line. Pressing on takes courage and it takes discipline. We will encounter times in this life when it's painful and we just don't feel like going any further. It is important in those times to draw strength from His Word and courage from focusing on the big picture to keep us moving forward.

I Am Unworthy

Judas and Peter both betrayed Jesus. One allowed godly sorrow to drive him to repentance and back to the Savior. The other let guilt and shame drive him to damnation. Both men started their race in the same way, but only one finished well.

The disciples were all gathered in the garden the night of the betrayal when a mob of soldiers and religious leaders came with swords and clubs in hand. They were looking for a rabbi by the name of Jesus of Nazareth. Among those coming to arrest Jesus, there stood a man named Judas leading the pack. Judas was one of the original 12. He was personally chosen by Jesus to be an apostle. He left everything to follow Christ over 3 years ago. Judas was sent out with the others to preach the gospel. He witnessed all of the miracles of Christ first hand. He watched Jesus heal the sick, raise the dead, and cast out demons. He just ate the passover meal with Jesus and the other disciples hours prior, yet here he was about to betray the Son of God with a holy kiss. A symbol of love and devotion was about to be used to hand over Jesus to be humiliated and crucified.

During the passover, Jesus said, *"The Son of Man will go just as it is written about him, but woe to that man by whom the Son of Man is betrayed! It would have been better for him if he had not been born." Matthew 26:24.* When the soldiers went to arrest Jesus, one of his disciples pulled out his sword and cut the ear off of the high priest's servant. Jesus told his disciple to put away the sword and proceeded to submit himself to the chief priests. This disciple's name was Peter. Peter was a man full of zeal, and had vowed hours earlier that he would lay down his life for Jesus if he had to.

Peter followed the crowd that arrested Jesus from a distance. Pretty soon, he was recognized as being one of Jesus' followers and denied it. He was questioned a couple more times and denied to even know the man and then a rooster crowed. Jesus looked over at him and it was then that he remembered what his master said earlier that night. *"Before the rooster crows, you will deny me three times." Matthew 26:34.* Peter couldn't bear the weight of what he just did and *"went outside and wept bitterly." Luke 22:62.*

The next morning, Judas was full of remorse and guilt seeing that Jesus had been condemned. He went to return the money he accepted to hand over Jesus the night prior. He told the chief priests that he had betrayed innocent blood, but they did not care. Judas threw the silver into the temple and went off to hang himself.

Fast forward to after the crucifixion and resurrection. Jesus sits at the right hand of the Father and sends the Holy Spirit to empower his followers to do His work. Time goes by and the followers of Christ are growing rapidly. Many were being harassed, persecuted and arrested for their faith in Jesus. The believers met in secret, fearing the public gatherings. As they were all gathered together getting ready to celebrate their risen Lord, word comes that James the brother of John had been arrested and beheaded. The times were increasingly wicked and there was no tolerance for anyone who proclaimed Jesus as Messiah.

Shortly after, Peter was arrested and sentenced to death. Bound by chains in a dungeon surrounded by armed guards, he gets a visitor. An angel of the Lord appears and miraculously releases Peter from prison. Peter goes to a home where many believers are on their knees praying for his release. When he knocked at the door, they did not let him in because they didn't even believe it was him.

Soon after, king Herod dies and Peter remains in Jerusalem as a leader of the church. Eventually, Peter travels to Rome to minister to the believers in that area. Nero was a very wicked Roman ruler who hated Christians. He determined to have Peter executed. Before capturing Peter, word got back to him in time to flee the city. As Peter approached the city gate, he saw Jesus walking in the other direction.

Falling to his knees, he cried out, *"Lord, where are you going?"*. Jesus replied, *"I've come to be crucified again"*. Peter took this to mean that his race was finished and turned back into town. Years prior, Jesus prophesied how Peter was to die saying, *"When you were younger, you would tie your belt and walk wherever you wanted. But when you grow old, you will stretch out your hands and someone else will tie you and carry you where you don't want to go."* John 21:18.

Upon being captured and sentenced to crucifixion, Peter said he was not worthy to die in the same manner as his Lord. Instead, he requested to die on the cross upside down. The Romans honored his request, and Peter went home to be with Jesus.

Not Alone

You are not in this alone. You have brothers and sisters all around the world who are struggling day-to-day to live out what they believe. It is a battle to keep our focus on Jesus, but it's a battle worth fighting. When you feel you have done all you can do to stand, stand firm. What consumes your mind will control your life. That is why it is so important to fix our eyes on Jesus. *"You will seek me and find me when you search for me with All Your Heart." Jeremiah 29:13 (my emphasis added).* Keep seeking Him and persevere to grab hold of the prize. The prize of Jesus.

"I have fought the good fight, I have finished the race, I have kept the faith. There is reserved for me the crown of righteousness, which the Lord, the righteous Judge, will give me on that day, and not only me, but to all those who have loved his appearing." 2 Timothy 4:7,8

Jesus frees us to live a life of true purpose so that we can finish well in Him. He frees us from the treadmill of productivity, performance, and perfection. In the end, the only thing that will matter is what we did for Jesus. The only thing that will matter is that we received His grace and mercy and extended it to others. All else will fade away. So be free and finish well!

Jesus Frees Us

The acceptance of forgiveness and the free gift of salvation is not the end, but the starting line to living a resurrected life in the fullness and freedom of Christ. Jesus died so that we can live. He brings us from death to life and lives His life through us. If in the reading of *Jesus Frees Us*, you have decided to give your life to Christ and start living in the freedom that only He can bring, or if your life has been impacted in another way through the ministry of this book, then I would love to hear from you.

May God bless you with an overwhelming awareness of His presence in your life and a continual hunger to know Him and experience Him in deeper ways.

I can be reached at JesusFreesUsTN@yahoo.com

Made in the USA
Monee, IL
01 July 2020